CW01500719

Emails from Ireland

Johann Wentzel

CreateSpace

Cover design: **Jaco Strydom**

Printed and bound by: **CreateSpace**

Almost anything you do is insignificant, but it is very
important that you do it.
Mohandas Karamchand Gandhi

Guess what?
Very few people actually "read" emails!

Linda, you have got mail
(and a few stories).

Inbox

Readme   x

Contacts   1

1. **Subject:** Ireland / My first two weeks   3

2. **Subject:** Ireland 11/08/2006   7

3. **Subject:** To beer or not to beer   11

4. **Subject:** Me again – from a beautiful wet…   13

5. **Subject:** Johann the NI philosopher   17

6. **Subject:** a Cold drink is not a liquid   21

7. **Subject:** A bit of this, a bit of that, …   25

8. **Subject:** So we went shooting – clay pigeon…   29

9. **Subject:** Master Jack   33

10. **Subject:** The ship docked outside is the Bounty   35

11. **Subject:** And even the flies are civil and lazy   39

12. **Subject:** Leipoldt must have been in Ireland…   41

13. **Subject:** Follow-up on "Leipoldt must …"   45

14. **Subject:** The house in Bready Northern Ireland…   47

15. **Subject:** On a Friday afternoon   49

16. **Subject:** Christmas in Ireland   53

17. **Subject:** Singing in the snow, dancing…   57

18. **Subject:** Salt salt everywhere and not a pinch... 59

19. **Subject:** So I am off to Passo Tonale Italy 63

20. **Subject:** 17 April 2008 65

21. **Subject:** 90 Pounds Sterling later and... 69

22. **Subject:** Form the new offices at Springpark... 73

23. **Subject:** My sentimental email 77

24. **Subject:** I am and therefore I must be... 81

25. **Subject:** Autumn has arrived as has... 85

26. **Subject:** And 'they' are concerned about... 89

27. **Subject:** No news 91

28. **Subject:** A song, a history lesson and some... 93

29. **Subject:** Bready NT82 0EQ 97

30. **Subject:** Digging my grave with my teeth 101

31. **Subject:** Friday the 13th and an hour to go! 103

32. **Subject:** *Ty is gebore en ek wil skoon flou word!* 105

33. **Subject:** So my first grandchild (grandson)... 105

34. **Subject:** Summer has sprung! 107

35. **Subject:** Snakes, fleas and the Irish 109

36. **Subject:** Spring has sprung - again 111

37. **Subject:** All the 'S''s 115

38. **Subject:** It is hot 119

39. **Subject:** RE: Greetings from South Africa 123

40. **Subject:** My kingdom, my kingdom for a… ... 127

41. **Subject:** Friday's thought 131

42. **Subject:** What a terrible game of Rugby 133

43. **Subject:** Just listen 135

44. **Subject:** My daily drive to work 139

45. **Subject:** Wednesday's thought 143

46. **Subject:** It's a strange strange world… 145

47. **Subject:** Isn't it strange that the strange… 149

48. **Subject:** So I killed the swallow! 153

49. **Subject:** An Irish winter's tale 157

50. **Subject:** Early Christmas wishes 161

51. **Subject:** Belfast - the new chapter 163

52. **Subject:** A burst water pipe, a flooded house… 167

53. **Subject:** I think too much 173

54. **Subject:** It could have been Ireland 177

55. **Subject:** 1 March 2010 183

56. **Subject:** It is Thursday - Friday for me this week 185

57. **Subject:** But Newcastle in Northern Ireland… 189

58. **Subject:** Floods and other animals   195

59. **Subject:** Or is it?   199

60. **Subject:** To be or not to be / To email or…   203

61. **Subject:** October / *Oktober* 2010   207

62. **Subject:** Sometimes I just sit   211

63. **Subject:** No, I don't know but   215

64. **Subject:** Hot of the press!   219

65. **Subject:** Werner Wentzel - 20 Nov 1974 to…   223

66. **Subject:** Get your dress made - we are flying…   225

67. **Subject:** To the Bride-to-Be from the lucky…   227

… The wedding vows   229

And the first three stories   231

Vonkpos uit Ierland

68. **Subject:** *Johann W – Ierland*   *247*

69. **Subject:** *Sommer bietjie nuus*   *251*

70. **Subject:** *Lekker weer*   *255*

71. **Subject:** *Ierland Maandag 22 Oktober 2007*   *257*

… To be sure to be sure   261

Readme

I landed at Dublin airport early on Wednesday, the 26th of July 2006. I turned 54 that August, August 2006.
Don't ask me why. Don't ask me why I came to Ireland less than a month before my 54th birthday.
The answer may just depend on what the weather was doing at the time of asking, or what I was eating, or how much sleep I had the night before or how the Irish or Ulster Rugby team was playing.
What I might have thought (that I know), was that I may just get on the plane and go back to South Africa whenever I felt like it, but not today. Not even today nearly five years on.
I will be 59 this August, August 2011.

I had a job offer in July 2005 at roughly half of what I was then earning back in Sunny South Africa. I started working in Londonderry / Derry / The Walled City, Northern Ireland on Monday the 31st of July 2006. I did not know then that Londonderry / Derry / The Walled City is the same place.
I also did not know that all the jokes about potatoes are true. There are still many things, about this most beautiful country in the world, that I don't know.

I do however know that I am here to stay.
I knew that from that moment when I declined the offer to go back to South Africa. That was about six weeks after first setting foot in Ireland. It took me less than a second to decide. It was not necessary to even think about it. The plane has taken off without me.

It is so simple: life does not have a reverse gear.

X

Contacts

Adam
Alan
Alison
Alta
Anne-Marie
Aria

Bill
Brenda
Brian

Carolyn
Caryn
Chris
Christo
Clive

David
Derek
Dries

Eddy
Elaine
Elbereth
Elna
Elsa

Faried
Flip

Frank
Freddie
Frikkie
Fritz

Gabriel
Gani
Garth

Henry
Herman

Izan

Jacques
Johan
Johann
Juan
Julie
JW

Karen
Kotie
Kim

Lariza
Larry
Lesley
Limont

Linda
Louise
Lutz

Maggie
Marinette
Mark
Martin
Michael
Monica

Paul
Peter

Renier
Rolf
Romeo
Ronald

Seray
Shane

Teena
Tony

Wilna
Wynand

Yusuf

1

Friends, family and others .

It is not a public holiday in Ireland, but then, I am getting 25 days annual leave, plus another six public holidays, plus "hours" off work (ten hours a year) for "things" and parental leave and and and...

I have settled, had the apartment's curtains washed and it shrunk about 12 inches, so now I don't only have a sun that only sets at 11, but also a daylit bedroom when I go to sleep. It is a fully furnished place, including, now shorter, curtains.

I walk and walk and walk: a bit like Johnny Walker, only thing is, I walk more or less the same route everyday: to and from work, the pubs (have developed a short-lived taste for potatoes (chips), potatoes (curry), potatoes (skins), potatoes (champ), potatoes (mash) potatoes (potatoes) and also Guinness. I tried to keep up with the Guinness but gave up after three outings, will have half of a half-pint and then swap glasses. My stomach / liver / age can't seem to handle it. I only managed the potatoes for two days. Have decided to settle for any "side order", even asparagus, rather than more potato. One has to appreciate it, your meal comes with some potato standard anyway. What I am talking about is the additional "side" that one is entitled to. And I walk...

Interesting people. Not only do they leave their cars outside, but sometimes even their children in pushchairs. I found this so interesting that I took a photo of a baby in his / her pushchair outside a building (on the pavement next to the front door). I was laughing at this, so the parents must have heard and came to have a look, and they don't speak real English. Were quite offended that I paid "undue" attention to their offspring.

Nobody speaks English, some "sing", some swallow their words, but nobody speaks English. They sing songs in their pubs in English but they don't speak English.

And they stay within the rules - you should see the paper associated with work, but they don't speak English. I have however taught a few some Afrikaans already: things like "*buy-a-donkey*".

And I walk and open doors... All doors are "spring loaded" and shut on you if you are unlucky, or behind you if you are lucky. All doors are fire doors, even the doors in the apartment close by themselves, you have to fight them open. First thing that I did was to buy doorstops (six!) to keep the flippen doors open. My biceps have grown about two cm just trying to keep doors open for people to get in / out.

Then there are naked ladies on page 3, Prince Charles is bigger news than the Middle East and I could not watch the Rugby. I did however wear my Bok windbreaker to work on the Friday.

Will have to get a car. Taxis are not too bad – it is basically £2.50 per trip in town and about 4 pounds when you leave the city borders. Food is expensive but maybe because I tend to eat out a lot. I have not yet got the hang for ironing, but do take out the garbage, vacuum the floors, make the bed and lay the table for breakfast. I am within easy walking distance (do I have a choice?) from work and tend to go back to the apartment for lunch ever so often. The shower runs off electricity and the rest of the hot water off gas. Had to pay a 200 pound deposit for gas but no deposit for phone or electricity. Places still accept cheques.

The weather, interesting... rain, sun, mist, rain, sun, rain and that only during my eight to ten minute walk to work in the morning. Start work at 9 and leave at half past six. Knock off at 16:15 on a Friday. Work is not a killer - everything is done according to very detailed guidelines. There are "formal" tea breaks, lunchtimes, work-hours, callout procedures, HR, etc. etc. etc. time off work, family matters. You name it and there is paper governing it. The people go out of their way not to be in your way, except in the pubs - "*hoe later hoe kwater*" - lots of noise.

Driving is something else: all cars have to be roadworthy. Cars older than 4 years are tested annually, everybody has insurance and people give way to let others in (apart from me, I still try and fight for my piece of the road). Very few BMW's on the road, so that may explain the lack of road rage. I tried to make sense of their banks and car financing. Could not, cars are financed at an APR of 6,4% or 5.9% if you go for a residual value and that is it. If you want to negotiate a different rate then you have to get a personal loan. Lots of other costs associated with cars, as mentioned, all cars must carry insurance and then there is road tax based on engine size and whether diesel or petrol.

Cable / satellite TV is pricy, more than 15 pounds a month for the cheapest sky option. Phone calls to South Africa (cell phones) are horrific, but here are ways of getting round that - phone cards.

"Groete vir almal" and may the Boks win a game, any game.

From: Johann Wentzel
Sent: Fri 11/08/2006 13:47
2. Subject: Ireland 11/08/2006

I have discovered that certain things work and others should be left alone.
"Royal Mail" works, alcohol free beer, well rather have a wee cuppa tea.
Posted a cheque to the Gas company in Belfast (about 100 km from L'Derry) late on Friday. Had a handwritten receipt delivered via post to the door on Wednesday morning.
Had a Beck's AF - Alcohol Free beer and woke up with a headache.

The cheque has not yet been cleared through my bank - banks are sloowww. Have to wait three plus weeks for an appointment to open a bank account. Was told that they will be quick - should have my ATM card within two weeks after opening the account! Balance may take up to three days before it is updated and reflected on your statement!

Johann's history lesson on Londonderry.
Two groups - one group likes the English but hates the Brits. The other lot hates the Brits but respect the English. Come to thing of it, The Irish are a bit like the Afrikaners! The Protestants want to be part of Brittan and call Londonderry that, Londonderry. The Catholics want to be on their own and call Londonderry, Derry. But then I may be 100% wrong, it may just be the other way round.

The Catholics support Celtic (green jerseys) and the Protestants the Rangers (blue). But again, I may also be 100% wrong on this one.

The "Derry Taxis" are reluctant to go into the protestant area and will take the sign on their cars' tops down if you give them ample warning else they may run the risk of being stoned.

There are a few "hoods" around - hooligans that drink (mainly over weekends) and break bottles. That seems to be the extent of their crime. And that makes the papers - front page. House stoned and bedroom window broken, only the first pane of glass (everything is double glazed) cracked. Headlines screaming that the cops must act immediately - attempted murder case to be opened and investigated. (I forgot to lock the front door last night (Wednesday) and only realized it when I left for work at 10 to nine this morning. But then, I do have double doors - main door into the complex (nine units - three to a floor and I am on the middle floor) and my own front door.)

Have also been to two key-cut places to have a second set of keys cut - it is the same key for both the complex and the apartment's doors and were told "no go".

It is a security key as it can open more than one access door and I will require written approval from the owner / agent / governing body / Protestants / Catholics before it can be done. Not that they don't have the equipment, it is just not done without the paperwork.

Then, the dear ironing. We South Africans must be wrong, wearing the same clothes only once and ironing everything.

But, I am not complaining. The place / people / businesses / work / university (our offices are on the Magee campus) are more than what I expected. Also a lot more time on my hands but appreciate that this may change in winter. Unbelievable view from my desk - looking out over the Foyle River.

Missing the children (*baie baie*) and a select few individuals and the TV sport channels.

Not missing work (pressure & callout) at The Bank, the hawkers, car watch, kombi taxis, heat, beggars, hours in the traffic, noise, cutting grass (not that I did that – hay fever), cleaning the pool, collecting post, driving to the shop, power failures...

Do I sound like a real pain?? a real ex- SA? Actually hoping that I may be followed by those few select individuals.

Regards.

View of the Foyle River from my desk as seen by my cell-phone (or "mobile" as it is known here):

It was the best of times, it was,
I am still having a good time.

Ek het gou afgeleer om Guinness te drink - miskien weer eendag in die toekoms - as Andrew kom kuier.

And they don't know what a semi sweet white wine is - will bring you a Rosé.

Then, they even have chips with Chinese. Beautiful fantastic Chinese place that we have been to - twice - and you can have "curry-chips" with your Chinese. Also went to Letterkenny to go and have curry chips at the 4 Lanterns. Ended up with two large portions of garlic chips! All Ronald and Aria's fault!!

Did I / Do I experience teething problems?
A few, but too few to mention. Must be a song in there somewhere...

Will I encourage / suggest it to others?
Beslis / definitely.

Will I take responsibility for anybody making the move?
No ways!

Put anybody up?
For a couple of days and then they go! I am selfish like the rest of the people here. Things work as they are so don't fix

11

it.

And the couple is the English couple – two! People that love ironing may get a stay...

Why?
It depends on what one wants. It did cost me a lot of money and I don't think I will ever recoup that, but I knew that from before I got onto the plane. And I never had that much to lose anyway. I am still stuck with the house and car in JHB.

I have gained a lot - more time. More time and more freedom. It is a relieve to be able to walk, drive, do your own thing, park anywhere and get wet. Not to worry about interest rates going up, the price of petrol, the Rand going down. The Rand does not even feature in news reports. Driving the latest car, getting to work on time. Traffic not giving way, not stopping at traffic lights or crossings. That your place may get burgled while you are out. I am staring to sound like a real, real what, asshole?

What do I miss the most?
The children (I have to say that) and Spur, the Bulls losing and proper meat but I guess I will still find a butcher that may be able to solve this little problem and I may just one day get SKY and be able to watch SA rugby.
O ja, and the Sunday papers - the gloom & doom and the back page.
Maybe the sun but not yet. Afrikaans, but I am teaching them a few words. Less wet clothes in the apartment, but I am getting the hang of that.

Johann has left the country.

A paperless society based on paper! Everything, just about, is done online, but only if you have the paper to go with it / back it up / wrap it up / wipe it / prove it.

And I am still having it. Can't wait for winter. Want to see how the central heating works and whether there may be power failures, or slippery roads or cold gale force winds and mad Englishmen. And whether cars will be able to stop in time when I cross the roads. You press the button, wait for 'walk' and walk. I wave thank you (like the Queen), a short little wave and am told that I am mad thanking them - I do however keep the other people on the car side when I cross - just in case...

www.remax-ireland.com
Link above gives one an idea of 1) property prices and 2) what one may get for £140 000-00 plus, but don't let the price fool you - "*die lere doen dit anders*".
That is the starting price and one has then to put in an offer. Highest offer wins, I think.

Then there are council tax, gas and / or oil and electricity.
Cars sleep in the street.
Currently water is free but that is changing as from next year - and can the people complain about anything that may change their ways - like having to now pay for water.
Lots of the stuff around, water that is. Not the problems at home.

Went driving this weekend - covered about 150 miles – to sample more potatoes. This time curry chips and strawberry milkshake. Wonder why nobody has ever attempted to market curry chips in South Africa. And the Guinness does taste different depending on where you sample it but is always ice cold.

By the way, it is miles in Northern Ireland and km in the Republic of Ireland, Pounds north, Euro south, and no English is spoken in either but I did take the ferry to cross from the one side of the Foyle River to the other - a 10 minute trip - 7 pounds or 10 Euro.

No real news – I am actually starting to do some (proper) work, the L'derry football team played to a zero zero draw against some French team (best that any Northern Irish team has done in something like 72 years and 72 years is nothing in a country where they don't destroy things or rename towns / streets / squatter camps) and is playing in France towards the end of September - big excitement...

Shops are getting ready for Halloween, I must take leave before end of the year - any leave carried over into the new year will impact the paperwork. May even take a few days and go and support the Candy Strips (Derry team) in Paris!

Then, estate agents don't work, they collect. (Come to think of it, but anyway...) You phone them when you spot a "For Sale" sign, they contact the owner and arrange a time for you to go and see the owner and that is that, no follow-up calls, no 'may we show you other properties', nothing like that. I first thought is was only because I am Afrikaans maybe?, but have since discovered this is the Irish way.

You then find a mortgage and submit your offer and phone to find out whether there was a better offer and submit your offer and phone to find out, but none of that for me for now. Have decided that *we is what we is'*. We want service. We want to be nagged and driven around to go through other people's houses to see whether they also have clothes that don't want to dry hanging all over the place.

Either that or they don't wash.

Just about impossible to find a 3-bedroom place with 2 bathrooms - think you are mad when you ask whether the place has two bathrooms.

This is the life, but don't all rush to join me - can hardly handle the thought of the lady from (am I at liberty to already broadcast that?), anyway, there is a possibility of somebody actually pulling up her SA roots to start work here.

Regards.

Weird, but it is not for me to say who is weirder! Less than 10 meters to the little boy's room (at work that is). Three doors, four if one wants one's own cubicle. To the kitchen (at work) one floor - 7 doors one way plus a fridge door if you want milk. And that is one way - so 22 doors to open and close for one trip to the kitchen to get a wee cuppa tea if you stop on the way there and don't what to hang out with the other big knobs.

The people (country) are obsessed with fires and / or doors. All doors are fire doors - but the fridge. It may be because they use gas and / or oil to generate heat. Fire may be a problem. Can't wait for winter to start.

I have taken an interest in the gas meter / box - take a reading every week on a Sunday morning - like clockwork. Also the neigbours' meters. Want to see who uses more gas - me or them. Have a written record going back four weeks and I am using less gas even though I bath more. So, not only am I cleaner than the neigbours, I am also conserving energy.

This is an amazingly beautiful country, inhabited by good friendly and a bit naive people - child-like in the nicest of ways (not like the "child-like" lot north of the border in good old South Africa). Leave stuff laying around, and not only their children. The air is clear and clean, not so the streets. Tend to be papers and wrappers laying around but they do recycle glass, plastic and paper. More things like sweet

17

rappers and sandwich containers - the first world price for convenience. Interesting to see the cleaners that pick up - older and friendly while they work. The council also seems to actively involve (employ) people with disabilities - the one sweeper on our way to work is deaf and dumb, *maar wie werk is hy*.

Legend has it that a chieftain and his sons sailed past the green emerald. They were so impressed by the beauty of the country with its rugged shorelines and waiving green fields that the chief promised the land in front of them to the first son to lay a hand on it.

The two sons jumped into there boats and started rowing for land. After a few minutes the one son, realizing that he will never make it, drew his sword, chopped off his hand and with a mighty swing, threw it, with the other hand, obviously.

That was the first chapter in the bloody history of Ireland.

Back to the philosopher. Can God create a rock that He can't lift (and I am not talking about Os du Randt). Not even I have all the answers.

Did it cost me a hand? I would say more like an arm and a leg - what a cliché but could not resist the temptation! Werner, Michael, Elbereth and Marinette that stayed behind, even though they are adults and individuals in their own right.

What about when the grandchildren start arriving? I will most definitely miss out - my biggest (only) regret. What if crime or worse should catch up with them? One has to ultimately take responsibility for oneself, even if it is only to justify your own decisions.

Any other regrets? The money that it cost me? The South African way of life? The two car way of life? The easy drive to Spar? The *braais*? The pool? The Lions, Springboks? The friends that I left behind? (What friends?)

Ireland is a bit off the beaten track - it is easy to get to London from anywhere in the world, a bit more of an effort to get across to Ireland.

Did you know it is only something like ten miles (16 km) between Ireland and Scotland at one point? That one can actually see Scotland from around Giants Coarseway area?

Make no mistake, the 'English', they are different. Latest is that children, the current generation, are not allowed to be exposed to physical violence. The theory is that violence breeds violence and that the next generation will be without aggression / violence (maybe so that the ones with the towels around their heads can have it their way?). So no slapping, kicking, hitting, shouting at any child. And all children under 12 must now be strapped into a car seat. All children under 12 or shorter than 4' 5" - *dit is een vir Daantjie Desimaal.*

Off to Belfast: my first long trip by own car, in the next 20 minutes. Then a flight to London (Stansted) tomorrow (Thursday) evening.

Then back home, Londonderry (Derry airport) Sunday evening and back at work Monday morning 9 o'clock.

By the way, the flight to Stansted airport less than £40-00 pp return with Ryanair.

Frasier has left the building, or was that Elvis? Not even I have all the answers.

A cold drink is not a liquid - a la any nearly eleven year old scientist.

But a lipstick is dangerous to civil aviation (a la the civil aviation over ten know-all scientists) and a small extra bag will put you back 7 pounds (or about R100-00) for the hour's flight from Stansted to City of Derry airport.
Two extra (small) bags - £14-00 and M & M will be visiting in December.

Dit gaan nog steeds klopdisselboom hier (a *disselboom* can be an Afrikaans band (actually the band is called *dissselblom* - well worth listening to their music); it is also that thing running from the wagon between the oxen and the wagon - and a wagon that really motors, will cause the *disselboom* to knock). So anyway, it is going *punt-in-die-wind* here in Londonderry - nights are getting longer and the days are getting colder. No need for the central heating as yet but there is more and more condensation against the windows in the morning – breathing. The clothes are taking longer to dry so I am wearing less clothes in the house.

Getting from here to the main land (how can an Island claim to be a 'main land'?) is a problem. Less than 20 km (if you are willing to swim and you may end up in Scotland) but it might as well be 20 thousand miles. Flights are cheap but exhausting - to airport, to bus, to train, to airport, to train, to bus, to airport, to home. And you have to allow for bags being hand searched because there is a full sealed bottle of cold drink in it. The cold drink is confiscated, the bag is searched, the inside of the bag is swapped and the swap analyzed ... Lipsticks (and other cosmetics) end up in the bin. Ditto for lighters, matches, scissors, shaving cream...

So, thank heaven for the difficulty to get to Ireland and ultimately Londonderry, it keeps people away. May that never change. I am selfish!

Londonderry is a young wife in an ageless body - I am in love. I am jealous - don't want everybody to know about the most beautiful city in the world. The view, she bursts out all over, her pulse, her weather and her demands. Her heart beats with mine (or is it mine beating with hers?). She has got scars that she flaunts, she is unpredictable; sun, rain, fog and she rushes you along, find you wherever you try to hide. She has worn down many over the years, seen many come and go, has cried and laughed, but she will never let go. She will surprise you when least expected. Her eyes are clear and her breath fresh. She does not pretend; a mixture of old Cape Town and a clean downtown Johannesburg - colourful houses down narrow uneven streets opening up in green parks; new next to old, small next to big, sharp corners when you expect a dead-end, cul de sac when you don't, young fathers pushing prams, dads dropping kids at school, taxis waiting for you to cross the street, cars flashing lights to give you way, what more can I say?

It is ten minutes over the hour of two, the sun is shining and there is an oceangoing trawler moving down (up?) the Foyle River, less than two hundred meters from where I sit. People on board getting ready to dock not 400 / 600 meters from where we work.

I just had a full breakfast including black & white pudding, lasagna, chips and salad and hot tea out of a mug - total cost less than £4-90. I also spent an hour in the post office - assisted by a post office employee that lent me a pair of scissors to cut photos, scotch's tape and envelopes to be paid when I get back and lots of advice / an explanation of what to do and what to expect.

Have just posted all my personal documentation, all the originals: passport, ID. employment offer, letter of employment, bank statements - in other words, my all. Why, to apply for a residency permit. I should know in a few weeks, till then, don't get ill, die or expect me to leave the UK - I can't. I am stuck.

A cold drink is not a liquid, but then, who really cares, the people in the queue behind you at the post office are patient - their turn will come. I left my cell phone (Saturday) on the counter at the Laundromat and went to look for it half an hour later - it was waiting. With a note to say that it should be kept with the washing to be returned to me on Wednesday when I come to collect the ironing.

Will I ever get use to a world where everything and everybody is controlled? I honestly don't know.

Even the Christmas drinks - only six free drinks per person and then you start paying. Paying for extra bags because that is the rule? Not raising your voice when you get cross? Not having to clean-up after the cleaner? Having to register with a doctor, dentist? Paying road tax every six months? Car roadworthy every year? Reporting on emergency hours off work (10 hours a year max)?. Back-to-back episodes of

Friends / Everybody loves Raymond / Frasier ? Seinfeld / Simpsons / etc / etc. Getting to trust the postal service? A telephone that does not work if there is ever a power failure?

I honestly don't know.

May it never change - I am selfish, in love and just a little bit jealous and for now, stuck in paradise.

From: Johann Wentzel
Sent: Tue 27/03/2007 17:40
7. Subject: A bit of this, a bit of that, something borrowed, something blue, but nothing old

I had a question (two) from one of my last remaining friends (maybe only remaining friend) in South Africa.
Anyway, the questions were - *still enjoying it?* and *what is your account number?*
The second question is easy and a pleasure.
WJ Wentzel
ABSA
and nobody has to wait for my 55th birthday on the 24th of August of this year.

The other question: *Still enjoying it?*
Very much so, just a wee bit hot at the moment - 4 o'clock in the afternoon. Then, the cricket is interesting and just wait for the Rugby World Cup... I just had a quick walk home to get out for a couple of minutes - with the excuse to collect a few work related notes from home. Takes less than 15 minutes there and back.

The sun has been shining since Friday, so we must be due for some rain. Will have to get sunblock (mustn't forget that. Can forget everything else...). We also set the clocks back on Sunday so there is now only an hour difference between us and S.A., but it is still light until about 9 at night!

I have this terrible habit to get up at three in the morning, watch TV, check my emails at home and just wander around - can't sleep. Get back in bed at about five and sleep for two hours (if I manage to fall asleep) get up at 07:30 to prepare breakfast and then get ready for work. Normally here at work at about 9 or shortly thereafter. Then lunch some time between 12:00 and 14:00 for about 45 min or an hour. Back at work until five thirty. Then off to the shops / home / walking / strolling next to the river / whatever at half past five and off to bed at about ten, ten thirty or there about.

Sleep late on Saturdays (even though can't...) and go for breakfast in town (found this place that serves steak, eggs and chips and the owner has been to S.A. in the early nineties when he stayed in Hillbrow, did the tourist things like Garden Route and Kruger Park) - walk to the restaurant, get out into the country, drive to the seaside - Portrush is a beautiful town with a nice beach about an hour or so away (too cold to even feel the water) and then the same on Sundays. Except that Sizzlers is not open on Sundays. No shops open until 1 o'clock on a Sunday (I don't go to church but enjoy the church bells that carry on for minutes at 9 and 12 - the tunes change depending on the time of year and the clocks actually tell time).

There is a Sainsbury's, a M&S and a Tesco, all within easy walking distance. Also KFC, McD, Chinese and the few Pizza places. Quite a number of pubs, but I don't drink, so ... One can walk home from the movies at midnight etc etc etc. really boring boring boring but I am enjoying it.

I would like to move a bit out of town (refer the answer to question one above) - firstly to get a bigger place and secondly to enjoy the country a bit more - it really is very green and clean and lots of lazy white sheep; all it seems, with twin lambs at the moment, little single lane roads with shrub fences higher than the cars and houses built right onto the road. Friendly people that give way and ask you how you are and your grandfather on mother's side and who are more than willing to volunteer their PIN numbers if you should bother to ask.

Our city - Londonderry

"The most visibly striking historic feature of the city is the historic walls. It is the only remaining completely walled City in Ireland and one of the finest examples of Walled Cities in Europe and they have been kept in a splendid state of preservation. The Walls were built by The Honourable The Irish Society as defences for early seventeenth century settlers from England and Scotland - the settlement was a plan of Plantation by James I. The building of the city was financed by the trade Guilds of the City of London and work began in 1613 and finished in 1618 under the supervision of Sir Edward Doddington of Dungiven.

The prefix London was thus added to the name of the city and the city of Londonderry became the jewel in the crown of the Ulster Plantations. The Walls which are approximately 1.5 km in circumference form a walkway around the inner city and provide a unique promenade to view the layout of the original town which still preserves its Rennaissance style street plan to this day.

The four original gates Shipquay, Ferryquay, Bishop and Butcher gates have all been rebuilt and three new gates added Magazine, Castle and New Gate. There are canon mounted throughout the Walls most notably above Shipquay Gate. These were donated by the Guilds of London in 1649.

Guided tours available all year round."

From: Johann Wentzel
Sent: Fri 15/06/2007 15:14
8. Subject: So we went shooting - clay pigeon shooting...

And I won - a trophy *"nogal"* - big silver cup with bluish tint - got 21 out of 25 and ended up with a bluish bruise on my right upper arm/shoulder. The right arm that is getting bigger and stronger due to the fire doors and my good manners. Am starting to look like one of those galley slaves that the Romans (?) chained to row their boats - growing skew and lopsided from working the one side more than the other.

And I am still walking, getting better at that as well - have even started overtaking the locals, an old dear with a walker just the other day and three men carrying a piano this morning.

And the potatoes - can't do without that either anymore. Just shows how adaptable we Afrikaners are – as they say: *"we is what we is."*

And I should be moving into my house next week this time or then at least have the key(s) in my sweaty little hands. That is painful and not to be recommended to anyone!! House buying in Northern Ireland that is.There is nothing like occupational rent in this part of the world. You may enter into a caretaker's agreement so that you may move in earlier (maybe) but only if and when all monies have been paid or something - I could not work out what that something is. We poor mortals must follow the rules and the rules are: All papers must be signed, the money must not only be released by The Bank, it must physically be in the solicitor's hand - left hand - and only then will the keys be handed over

- with the right hand (the strong hand). No prove of funds or prove of payment or flood of tears is good enough. I had to organize to have the funds released by Alliance Leister (building society) on Thursday next week so that the funds will be there Friday morning so that I may collect the keys on Friday after they have seen the money. Even bank proof signed in blood by all parties concerned that the money was released and available, is not good enough. Get the point? There is no flippin point and I told the solicitor so and got a £100-00 deduction in their professional fees for service that was not so professional. But then, one actually feels bad to complain about anything - the people are so unlike the Brits - they are 'nice', but still - I made the offer for the house towards the end of April, had proof of funds a few days later and actually paid £100-00 towards solicitors costs on the 1st of May to get the ball rolling and only had confirmation of a tentative *completion* date (that is what they call the money / hand shake / key routine) last week Friday and only after I insisted that I see the solicitor at 4 o'clock that Friday afternoon!!

And the sun. No wonder that Queen V. said that the sun never sets on the British Empire. The sun does not set, full stop / *punt* / *sela*. You go to sleep from pure exhaustion while the sun is shining brightly (11 at night) and get up exhausted while the sun is shining brightly (at 4 in the morning) to get into the car and drive pass filling stations that are not open (all family owned and run), no 24-hour convenience stores, no people on the streets but lots of children's toys, bicycles and clothes laying outside, no beasts prowling at traffic lights - just peace and quiet, winding single lane roads and sheep and cows and the smell of liquid sh*t that they spray over everything where one may possibly be able to plant a potato, drifting in the fresh morning air. This is the life. Maybe we Afrikaners are not the chosen race, but then, we are God's gift to the world. Such a pity I had that little operation all those years ago. Imagine what I could have done to the local blood line…

Anyway, I got my cup - won by 4 points and only after the others were given some grace. I also got lost on my way there and had to follow a guy on a bicycle for the last two miles. I also got lost on my way back and then pretended that I was house looking in Buncrana rather than admitting …

Got home at about half past ten in the evening and the guy that came second (17 out of 25) was standing on his 2nd floor stamp size patio - (smaller) cup in hand shouting JOUHAAHN and waving his cup. He was also dressed in the bare minimum. The use of alcohol second only to the abuse of the humble potato.

This is a beautiful island, thank god for the pain to get from and to the "Main Land". Thank god for the cold weather that are keeping people away. (That is a misnomer, the cold weather - it was 30 plus degrees last weekend when I went to Bundoran and swam in the sea). Thank god for the lack of a quick means between "here" and the rest of the world. Thank god for that friendly individual that deposited money into my SA Florida ABSA Current Account - *doen so voort*!

Have a good weekend.

From: Johann Wentzel
Sent: Thu 12/07/2007 11:42
9. Subject: Master Jack

It is a strange world indeed:

Not only can you pull away when the light turns orange but the Christmas Roses bloom in June, but TG, I am finally in touch with my feminine side: I am retaining water – 5 litres (5 kg) over the last ten months. And I am retaining it under my chin, can feel it sloshing around when I shake my head – sort of developing it into a party trick: my 4th of July turkey impression. It then seems to seep down from there to dam around my waist.

Somebody *tactfully* suggested that I should maybe change to Weighless food, horrible stuff, except for the vanilla flavoured rice pudding. So I now have two small bowls of Weighless vanilla flavoured rice pudding every night before going to bed – giving me three points. Everybody (all the women and even the odd man here) seems to be collecting these Weighless points but it looks to me as if it's worth as much as my frequent flyers points – like The Bank's reward scheme – promising a lot but delivering very little. I have also started dreaming of green slime covered overflowing dams on a Free State farm; green slime changing into vanilla mud as it overflows, hitting the dry soil.

I know some dude in The Bible once murmured that there are three things, no four, that he could never phantom: The flight of a bird and the way of a woman and I can't recall the other one (two) deep male beer induced thoughts, but I do know that those forgotten ones were all addressed and explained in my generation's (the seventies) pop songs. And I now know the way of women as well – they cry to get rid of the retained water – and that the flight of the bird has everything to do with aerodynamics. But I do have a new question: How do those little bodies manage to excrete such a lot of sh*t. Birds that is, not women.

I have three swallow families nesting under my roof, crapping on my walls, my windows, my car and my 1 x 6 front stoep – feet that is, not meters. Depositing enough ghwano to fertilize my 5 by 8 lawn three times over every week. It not for the memories of my dear departed mother I would have hosed the nests down ages ago – I feel the same for their chicks as what I feel for the Rhino – if you can't survive, tough. Can't wait for winter so that they go and I can take down their nests and make it into Chinese soup to feed to the fat women in Londonderry.

But life in Ireland is good to me and I can't get enough of the new house – it is too beautiful for even the cover on a box of chocolates – life has really dealt me the choosy bits.

And then – it is my birthday on the 24th of August – fifty five I will be. At an age where presents start having a new meaning again – sort of going back to one's childhood, so just ask for my new address (the local postal services still impress me no end):

My ABSA bank account details have not changed.

Love to all - the next email will have photos of the new house.

34

From: Johann Wentzel
Sent: Fri 10/08/2007 16:00
10. Subject: The ship docked outside is the "**Bounty**" …

Today (Friday the 10th of August 2007) two weeks and I will be 55.
Scraping the barrel I am. Feeling sorry for myself I am, but not for too much longer – will be out of it before then, the 55 that is. But I have earned it for now and I will wallow in it for a few hours more…

This place is the best, still.

I had to stand in, had to deputize: team leader in charge of 15 spread over two sites (L'Derry & Belfast) for two and a bit weeks. Then, just as I have sort of recovered from the first stint, again for an additional few days.The work admin, she killed me - did not get time to brush my teeth, but that helped in keeping the people at bay.
http://news.bbc.co.uk/2/hi/uk_news/northern_ireland/693849 0.stm

So what did the nearly 55 years teach me?

Women: she is different – it took me a long long time to realize that but it is true!!

It was really an interesting journey to get to that destination. Is there anything left after that discovery – I don't think so but I will ask a woman.

For those that can open the above link – this is really the most scenic and most beautiful country (island) in the www.

This "old" ship is less than a hundred meters from where I am sitting at the moment – I am a wee bit below the masts on about the same level as the *Stars and Stripes* that she is flying at her rear and what a rear. I actually went to touch that.

Talking about a view to die (kill) for:
The view from my downstairs toilet looks out and up over the most amazing green hill spotted with sheep and lazy cattle (and my unkempt piece of garden still to be decided what to do with it – plant grass that must be mowed, put in flowers that need TLC or go half half with grass and stones on top of a weed-free membrane that will (hopefully) require less maintenance).

The fact that the downstairs toilet leads out from the kitchen is a British thing – it also allows you to multitask - to load the washing machine instead of reading the newspaper.

Anyway, there I am every morning, contemplating what to eat / do with the garden / my life, seeing that I have made this major discovery (there are really no more unknowns) and can therefore now concentrate unhindered on lesser things, looking towards this green green hill with cows that don't have to walk to graze – the grass grows as they eat it, white lambs chase-playing a game that will turn lesser men into vegetarians and my heart is scattered, broken, will never ever heal again, crying for something to fill this void (and I can't drink due to a wee little liver issue), totally deserted by man and beast I pine for my loss that was my own making – it is terrible to be a man, to be so totally stupid, to let the reason for your existence slip through your fingers.

It is the best of times it is the worst of times. Not even all the presents that will be delivered in the next two weeks – a bit later for those posted in S.A., can dull it.

This vast emptiness in my being that can swallow this country a few times over has drained me, left me with no questions nor answers.

The tears that could have floated the "old" ship have run its course and I am at a total loss – can't question (who?), can't explain (to who?), can't phantom the why?

And can't yet accept…

But then, I am a white Afrikaner male, one of God's chosen few and as they say "*we is what we is*".
There are still seeds to be sown, earth to be fertilized, maybe even a few lost souls to be shown the ways of man.

And talking about swallows – they have left the nest – two chicks that still come back at night (I think) but at least they drop their droppings somewhere else and no more on me, the Royal Mail postman (www.royalmail.com) or my front stoep. But the nest is coming down in the winter and will never ever go up again. Even I can learn a lesson. Even I can take a stand and get going, even if I have to break a nest (or egg) in the process. We are men and so were our fathers before us – we can fight even with our hearts ripped out.

By the way, and this is no justification or even an admission – I have also left a few broken hearts in my wake, but don't have to be remembered about that just yet at this time.

37

I am also receiving visitors, a couple from Sunny South Africa on Wednesday for five days, then again another couple in the middle of the first week of September and I do have lots of free accommodation with a brilliant view, plus a brand new manpowered Bosch manual lawnmower for anybody that wants to experience good liver destroying food and/or drink.

Regards to all.

Credit to BBC

And even the flies are civil and lazy – sort of don't want to offend. Killed two with one blow the other day – will have a belt made – *two with one blow.*

Will there ever be another – I doubt it but then who knows... I have met this very pleasant Irish lady – 48 years old, financially independent [*good] , good job [better], very caring, [even better] qualified scientist, [now we are getting somewhere, pse send income and balance sheet statements for a free unbiased opinion ... oh also photo of her and bakkie] with a 19 year old son that started university a week ago and she is mad about me! [I knew it was too good] And I? The feelings are mutual [now, love and lust are both four letter words starting with L and both have something going for them ... decide which category this falls into and which is more fun] and her mother 'loves' me. [they all do but leave the mother alone, chics don't appreciate that kind of thing]

Then, I have lost my passport: Went to Dublin last week Monday and Tuesday to visit the South African Embassy. Much easier to go to Dublin than South African House in London. Also wanted to experience the south of Ireland a wee bit. Was really good fun and well worth it.

Anyway, I should have a new passport in 2 to 4 months. No use getting a temporary passport as the Brits no longer accept that – apparently too much corruption with temporary S.A. passports (if you want to believe that)! The Brits (UK

Home Office) also not too pleased with me for losing my passport with UK VISA, so I have to go through the whole apply-VISA process again.

Work wise – busy but manageable. Much better work/home balance that what I have had for the past 55 years. Even time to go to the odd pub to watch the World Cup and be recognized by the barmen. Have also had time to travel this little Island – absolutely beautiful. Not Chapman's Peak or the Garden route will come close to it par for the weather.

Regards to all and may the BOKS beat the Kiwis.

*T.D. in his male wisdom!

From: Johann Wentzel
Sent: Fri 12/10/2007 16:59
12. Subject: Leipoldt must have been in Ireland when he said that *"Oktober is die mooiste maand"*

Hi all.

Indeed it is, the most beautiful month that is.

Not even cold that is, with lots and lots of leaves turning autumn colours, no power failures and the central heating kicking in for a few minutes early in the morning and/or later at night. Very cozy it is indeed.

I am well and doing well – Halloween is at the end of October (quite a big thing in this part of the country with lots of Scots visiting from across the water) – I wonder why the Scottish take such an interest in Halloween at Londonderry? It is also a time for lots and lots of drinking – fall over drinking. Second only to St Patrick's day drinking.

I have however decided to stay off the streets on the 31st – actual Halloween day. I am staying about 8 miles or so out of town in my little village of 47 houses and no shops and will rather give both the drunken masses and cordoned off streets a miss. Have my own Halloween at home – play a few tricks on the neighbours maybe.

The lady, Angela, next to me – I stay in a semi (and that means we share an outside wall that is therefore not an outside wall anymore but would have been an outside wall if it was not a semi) and my bedroom shares this outside wall that is not an outside wall but that would… Anyway, Angela, the old dear and I share a common wall between main bedrooms and she has had the soundproofing improved

41

between us. Added another three inches to her side of the outside wall that is not an outside wall but that would have been an outside wall if it was not a semi: The wall that would not have required additional panels (three times 1-inch panels) of soundproofing if it was not an outside wall doubling up as a shared semi- wall.

Should have seen the mess in her house – called me one night this week to come and have a look, I was already in my PJ's when she knocked on the door (not on the semi-wall). Blushed when I said she should come in while I get dressed and then took me to have a wee look at her main bedroom, the bedroom that is joined at the hips with mine.

What a mess, carpets lifted, building rubble and dust everywhere – poor thing. Anyway, she seems quite happy and I had to run back to my house and go and shout in both the main bedroom and the lounge while she followed me on her side of the wall – trying to make out what I was shouting – *"Die Bokke Bo – Die Bokke vir die Wêreldbeker"* *"Op die Vaal"* etc. etc. etc.

The old lady really likes me – I take her bin out first thing every Monday morning. We each have two bins (everybody has two bins and some people even three), a blue one for stuff that must be recycled and a grey one for other rubbish (plus a brown one for garden rubbish). Anyway, I took it on myself to wheel her bin out and back every Monday – it is about 200 yards to the point where the bins congregate on Mondays. Her bins do not have a number. Every other bin out of the group of 47 times 2 has a white number painted on but not Angela's bins. Her bin of the Monday has an orange ribbon tied to the handle. This ribbon is swapped

42

early early Monday morning so that the friendly neighbour (that's me) may know which bin to wheel to the main street. I then try to sneak her bin back at night but have only succeeded once so far (the Monday that I went home at lunchtime to sneak the blue bin back). She waits for me and then invites me in for tea, to fix her doorbell, to fix the TV, to get into the attic and to laugh at me, telling me the whole time that she knows I am only teasing her and there I am actually doing nothing, just eating all the snacks that she has laid out.

I also cut her 4 yard by 6 yard patch of grass while she walks next to me, talking while I struggle to breathe – it is a manual lawn-mover – cost £39-00 at Argos. Must tell you more about Argos – it is a place where you can buy anything from a catalogue but where you get most of the stuff immediately.

Angela has also introduced me to Wendy, a younger unmarried woman that works as a feeding lady at a school and that spends quite a few nights a week at Angela's place due to the distance from her school to her own place just outside Belfast, to an American missionary couple, to a preacher and his very very attractive wife (both qualified vets), to another retired missionary and his much younger wife that spent ten years in Durban working the souls of the blacks in Africa with, I guess no success and to an old farming couple that stays just down the road. Really interesting people the Irish and everybody has family in Donegal: Donegal being one of the counties in Ireland and very scenic, very beautiful all year round and not only in October. Leipoldt would have approved.

Still lots that I wanted to say but it is Friday, it is the semi-final on Sunday and I am going home.

May the Bokke win.

From: Johann Wentzel
Sent: Mon 15/10/2007 14:09
13. Subject: Follow-up on "Leipoldt must have been
in Ireland when he said that "*Oktober is die mooiste maand*"

It's Monday, the Bokke had a good win after what I thought was a shaky start and I am just a little bit restless. Don't ask me why, or rather, I am going to find out why I am restless and then tell anyway.

But then I do think I know why!
No challenges left – England is going to be a walkover and I am 100% happy with myself, my children, my life, my work and my environment. My carbon footprint is healthy, big and strong – leaving a nice imprint – remember I have two bins (anyway, let the Rhinos become extinct if they can't take care of themselves). Ditto the humans – I am fifty five and can retire in less than nine years.

I am getting around quite a lot – have made a few friends and my house is spotless with not too much furnisher or dust gathering k*kkies to clutter but enough of everything to be comfortable.

I keep my washing under control, don't do any ironing (my Bosch washing machine has an *Easy Iron* setting and so the Tumble Dryer as well) that leaves the shirts looking ironed, go away every weekend, eat well and well. The best is – no crime and the roads are narrow but fast and safe, I earn Pounds and spend Pounds (Sterling) or Euros or Scottish Pounds (same as Sterling but different pictures) or Irish Pounds (more strange pictures) – the shops take any currency but Rands (even after the weekend's win), am planning to go to Cambridge on the 8th of December 2007 for Elbereth's graduation, to S.A. end of March beginning April 2008 for Marinette's graduation, most probably skiing in Switzerland end of the year (2007) if I have a passport by then and I still have something like 14 days leave left that must be taken before the end of this year. Five days may be carried forward to next year (me being a foreigner) and then I may be able to "buy" an additional five days leave in 2008, giving me 35 days of leave. I can also work in hours to take an additional six days TOIL - time off in lieu (a day every two months or a half-a-day every month) and then the odd flexi day / half-day / hour if I need to take the time off due to work stress…

So, why am I restless? I guess the above answers it all.

Roll on Saturday so that Sky News can sulk about the way that the English lost the World Cup that nobody expected them to win in the first place anyway!

Regards to all.

From: Johann Wentzel
Sent: Fri 20/04/2007 15:51
14. Subject: The house in Bready Northern Ireland, about 10 km outside Londonderry / Derry / the Walled City

Features

- SEMI DETACHED HOUSE
- OIL FIRED CENTRAL HEATING
- PVC DOUBLE GLAZED WINDOWS & DOORS
- PINE PANELLED INTERNAL DOORS
- SECURITY ALARM INSTALLED
- FIRE ALARM
- CARPETS & BLINDS INCLUDED IN SALE

This is a three bedroom semi-detached property situated in a much sought after rural location in Bready. It is within easy commuting distance of all local towns.

It has been beautifully maintained by the current owners and we would recommend early internal inspection.

ACCOMMODATION COMPRISES:
HALLWAY With tiled floor, understairs storage, telephone point.
LOUNGE 12'8 x 17'7" (TO Widest Point) Having attractive fireplace, laminated wooden floor, telephone point, TV point.

KITCHEN/DINING 13'4" x 13'2" Having eye & low level units, tiling between units, 1 1/2 stainless steel sink unit with mixer taps, 'Candy' hob & underoven, extractor hood,

47

intergrated fridge/freezer, plumbed for a dishwasher, matching window pelmet, tiled floor, TV point.

UTILITY ROOM 5'8" x 7' Single drainer sink unit with mixer taps, low level units, plumbed for a washing machine, space for a tumble dryer, extractor fan, tiled floor.

DOWNSTAIRS WHB & WC Tiling around whb, tiled floor.
FIRST FLOOR
LANDING Having hotpress.
MASTER BEDROOM 16'2" x 10'5" (To Widest Point) Having TV point. EN-SUITE Having a fully tiled walk in 'Redring' shower, wc, whb with tiling around, extractor fan, tiled floor.

BEDROOM (2) 10'5" x 11' (To Widest Point) Having TV point.
BEDROOM (3) 8'8" x 10'4" (To Widest point) Having telephone Point, TV point.
BATHROOM Comprising of bath, whb, wc, fully tiled walk in power shower, partially tiled walls, extractor fan, tiled floor.

Loft area partially floored with larder and light.
EXTERIOR FEATURES
Tarmac driveway
Outside light & tap
Decking area to rear enclosed by fence.

£170 000-00 *eina*! Interest rate 5.1% but I may get it at 4.49% depending on where you go to get financing.
It is out of town, so more for less.

House prices have now risen for 17 months in a row so there may be a possible bubble burst on its way but then peace has come to Ireland and there are lots of people moving here and the lot here know how to breed!

48

It is Friday afternoon and I am exhausted, *moeg*, can't wait to go home.

Was a busy two weeks, fortnight, as the Brits would say.

Policeman was shot yesterday morning after dropping his child at school – not killed but serious in hospital. Shotgun to his face. Policeman is a Catholic and was most probably shot by 'one-of-his-own', i.e. by the dissident IRA as an example or to scare Catholics from becoming police officers or to re-stir the troubles of days gone by.

Just a bit of Ireland history – it was also twenty years yesterday since an IRA bomb exploded in Enniskillen killing eleven people. Enniskillen is a truly beautiful place about half an hour from where I stay: Took my car there for its annual MOT... Lots of water and big trees, mountains and very green.

Anyway: Quite an outcry from all sides about the shooting with more than 60 police officers on the scene, combing the area and talking to witnesses.
Interesting, It happened yesterday morning (Thursday) and the police was there today, again, at the same time as what it happened yesterday morning to question people that may have seen or heard something yesterday as they were going to work, shops, schools.

Was a busy week, well two weeks.

49

My boss is off work and so was her boss for the first week and I am deputising, standing in, killing myself with lots of meetings, admin and the like, including attempting to keep the staff of twenty both happy and gainfully employed.

Our customer, Allstate (an insurance company) is based in Chicago, so we have a time difference of 6 hours that does not always make it easier.

But this is still a beautiful country, even with the storms of the last 36 hours that have been pelting the British coast from the North. Awesome images on the TV.

We in Londonderry or then the village Bready where I stay just had strong winds (like JHB August winds). Also some rain but it is still relatively warm for this time of the year.

And I am keeping within my budget – not easy but I am planning to visit SA some time next year.

How to keep within your budget? Easy, I love potatoes and my friendly neighbour... (cares for me).

I was also invited to meet with a group of people (Linda's friends) last weekend and we had a dinner party for fourteen people – took enough food home to see me through to Wednesday evening. The group has been friends for many moons – some date back to school days. Really interesting mix of people.

Have another dinner tomorrow evening to meet her (Linda's) work colleaques: Will not be able to carry food away though. We are going out this time.

Will have to tell everybody more about Linda, I guess.
She is in her late forties, Irish, blonde and so nice to cuddle.
Loves me to bits (…) and will be coming with when I visit.

"Bready is a small village in County Tyrone, Northern Ireland. In the 2001 Census it had a population of 93 people and it lies within the Strabane District Council area."

The village is home to Bready Cricket Club.

Talk soon.

The house in Bready that Johann bought.

52

From:	Johann Wentzel
Sent:	Thu 27/12/2007 16:52
16. Subject:	Christmas in Ireland

So ek is terug in die land van die werkendes.

And what fun it is to be 'working' again after putting on eight pounds in weight - due to me conforming to the British tradition of eating at least 8 pounds of chocolates, a whole turkey and sprouts - don't ask me why the sprouts - I can only think it has something to do with colour on your plate as you don't see the bottom of the plate for at least three days - must be something to do with being either wise or a virgin.

Then the ham - soaked overnight in water to drain some of the salt, then roasted in the oven - only to be removed to be painted with honey and then some more roasting. This is eaten first warm and then cold - on the 25th, the 26th, the 27th... it was a big ham. Christmas pudding with brandy custard, mince pies with no meat but more brandy custard and lots of other stuff as in stuffings: fruit, meat, nuts.

By the way - Mother Christmas was good to me - I was spoiled rotten. But then I was good (or is that bad) as well.

Bottom point - I had an excellent break from work - firstly a visit to Cambridge for Elbereth's graduation on the 8th of December. That was interesting but cold like one can't imagine - standing outside the thousand year old church where the ceremony was held was so cold that I could be neither good nor bad.

The story (graduation) itself was all in Latin - the Brits are as nuts as their Christmas puddings / turkey stuffings, but my daughter was a real star. Anne-Marie was also in attendance - all the way from summer. I took my new lady friend (Irish girl) with and everybody got along like a house on fire. So, that was my two days in Cambridge.

Coming back from Cambridge, we moved on to Waringstown - a little village outside Belfast where I had a typical Irish eat-(and-drink)-until-you-fall-over Christmas preceded by doing nothing for the better part of two weeks.

Life is still treating me well - it is quite cold and it takes some getting use to the sun only rising at 08:30 to setting again before 4 o'clock, but there was heating oil in the tank to leave a good carbon footprint and lots of central heating, chocolate to fill the tummy and heaps of TLC. We Afrikaner males are indeed the blessed ones. She is really so good to me - I am very lucky (and happy).

Work is, well work. The normal ups and downs - we do however have a good work / life balance company policy in place. So much so that one can now buy additional leave - up to five days a year - in addition to the 25 days that I qualify for, plus now 12 flexi days a year for hours worked in excess of what is regarded as normal (37,5 hours a week) plus a few hours (10) emergency leave a year plus the two days that I am carrying over from this year (2007). Just a wee little snippet to get the lazy ones to use their brains - that relates to how may days and hours of non-work for 2008?

I must admit - money is tight but then I have no debt over here - have a house that is costing a bit too much as I am

54

only staying there a few days a week. Electricity comes to less that £30-00 a month as it is most of the time only me. 500 litters of heating oil is about £230 and that should see me through the winter. Rates and taxes (municipal) nearly £800-00 a year payable over ten months. Plus road tax, car MOT, etc.

Then, the price of food is horrific when converting to Rands - two deboned Christmas turkey breasts (1,8 kg) = £27-00 from Marks and Spencers. Petrol is currently £1.07 per litre but I fill my car over the border (that is in The Republic of Ireland as I stay quite close to the border - 90p a litre). I stay about six miles from a number of Republic of Ireland garages. Milk is about £1.15 a litre and a loaf of bread about a pound. No *boerewors*, biltong or *mieliemeel* but we do have Mrs. Ball's and lots of different curries and spices. I had a footlong Subway meal at lunch time today and that with tea came to £6-09. Also no armed response, medical extras and my car and house insurance are a pittance.

Marinette called - had her official results from RAU - or as it is now called, Johannesburg University this morning - got her degree cum laude and the graduation is in March 2008

Want to know more - just ask.

Have a good and safe New Year.

The view from the Bready house kitchen.

17. Subject: Singing in the snow, dancing in the snow, peeing in the snow

So Christmas came and went - not so the snow.
Late in arriving and still very much around.
I had a good Christmas and start to the 2008 New Year,

Things, that is life, sort of back to normal with lots of people not back at work - overhung, tummy bugs or colds. The tummy bug is quite interesting - and one is not suppose to come back to work for 48 hours after it stopped.

The photos:
1. Linda, her son Adam, her Mom and Dad and the Mom's friend Tom.
Linda 48, the Dad 83, her son Adam 19, the Mom 77 (had a hip replacement two weeks ago) and the friend 86. The Dad is the one the worst for wear.

2. Then outside my wee Bready house when I woke up on Friday morning - it snowed on and off the whole of Friday,

No New Year's resolutions but many plans and also a visit to South Africa - may be even two. Missing M & M too much.

Regards to all,

Enough to make your blood pressure rise. That and Jamie Oliver's chickens.

Rather buy free range chicks (a la JO) - they are only slaughtered after 77 days and not after 37 / 38 / 39 days depending on how fast you grow (if you were a chicken).
So what did Tesco do? Dropped the price of chickens to £1-99 and the farmers are already only making 3 pence on a chicken.
Anyway it is a nice day outside - sun shining and must be anything from 11 to 15 degrees.
I have a walk next to the ocean planned for either Saturday or Sunday, come hail, snow or rain.
Sort of let the salt water clear my mind a bit - it was a busy few weeks since the New Year has broken.

Life is still (always) treating me well - still love the Irish, even more so but that is a different story.
My passport is at the UK Home Office and may be there for anything up to 6 months - must have a new UK VISA / endorsement issued seeing that I lost the old passport (in the post so not really me). Need a UK residence VISA / UK Endorsement to get a Schengen VISA to go skiing in Italy towards the end of March. Six into two (months) don't go I know but then I am a white Afrikaner male and doors open for us - even when you still have to allow two weeks to get the Schengen VISA after the UK VISA / Endorsement....

I am also on a saving-the-world mission - my electricity bill was just over £30-00 for three months! Eating at the neigbour at least once a week, using other people's showers (part of the different story) really cuts down on the carbon footprint. Why do I mention this? Just my way of saying come and stay here - we have uninterrupted electricity and no water charges. The Brits are trying to get the Irish to pay for water but there is *"water water everywhere and plenty to drink"* so the Irish are refusing and only Afrikaners (maybe) are more stubborn than the Irish.

The idea is that all households will pay £10-00 a month for water for the first year, going up to twenty in year two and thirty in year three and there it will stay or until water meters are installed.

But the salt. Not only is life expectancy like 79 plus for males and 81 plus for females but we must cut down on salt to live longer - 4 out of 5 people in old age care centres suffer from dementia and retaining care workers are a problem. All care workers will rather go and work for Tesco's - the pay is better and you don't bump into an old dear in the middle of the night - asking you for directions to her room / what day it is.

Where was I? Oh, the salt. Anyway imagine biltong without salt, eggs, even bread must be baked with less salt. Beware, the salt police are checking. First time I saw a Breakfast Bap advertised, I thought it was misspelled and read Breakfast *"PAP"* as in Oats or mealiemeal porridge. Big was my surprise (and disappointment) - it is a bun (salty) with egg and bacon and everything else. Really good to line the old stomach and now these "baps" were declared unhealthy - too much salt. But it is not *"PAP"* and it is not as strange as it may sound. The Irish are close cousins to the Scottish.

It is Friday and I have a walk next to the ocean planned so I am signing off - have a good one.

The next email will (should) have more news on my new '*home*' and the pretty wee Irish Sunshine Girl. The house a red-brick double storey with a power shower and things that go bump in the night.

Regards to all and may the Irish win their Six Nation's game this weekend.

PS - Jamie Oliver is sponsored by Sainsbury's.
Tesco has a 30% share in the UK retail market and growing.

Bayview but more later…

Castle Rock but more later…

From: Johann Wentzel
Sent: Fri 21/03/2008 11:56
19. Subject: So I am off to Passo Tonale Italy

But the "snow-plough" will be back... hopefully lighter. NI is treating me well - have just about doubled in size in 20 months.

Anyway, have to be at Dublin Airport at 4 o'clock tomorrow morning - Saturday 22 March 2008. Flight departs at 6 o'clock and I must be on it. Dublin is about two hours from where I will be spending this night and that is about two hours from where I am sitting, typing while scanning the Foyle River about two hundred meters away. Sun shining and 'warm', must be about 11 degrees plus... Lunch is approaching - I have baked a *mieliebrood* for a friend that had an operation on Wednesday, so I will be having tea and bread with her in a few minutes.

Back to Dublin where I will be reporting tomorrow morning at 4 o'clock.
With my new passport, new UK Residence VISA (valid to Oct 2011), new Schengen VISA (multiple entry valid from 22/03/2008 to 22/09/2008), new skipants, borrowed glasses and old Springbok windbreaker. And I should be back in Northern Ireland on the 29th of March. Will only be back at work on April Fool's Day. Then another day off on the 11th of April - invited to a real Irish wedding on the Friday, off on the 6 & 7th of May to Bayview Hotel overlooking the Northern Ocean and then good old South Africa in September - another wedding, birthday and the Children at 'home'!

Dis Goeie Vrydag en dit gaan inderdaad goed met my.
Die huis staan nog na die gale force winds, *die sneeu en die koue. Daar is nog olie in die tank en ons, ek en Linda, het 'n lekker naweek in Edinburgh Skotland gehad saam met Elbereth en Barry. Interessant, Jack White word genoem as moontlike nuwe afrigter vir Ierland.*

In elk geval - sommer net 'n vriendelike email om te sê ek is met vakansie.

I will be at Passo Tonale, Italy and they have a webcam or two showing people falling about on the slopes...

Hi All.

Times must be good with winter descending on Sunny South Africa.

I hear nothing, see nothing, get nothing... but there is a new SPUR in Belfast (Belfast Northern Ireland that is). Also a Nando's. Have been to the SPUR but not Nando's - can't do everything in one go. What will I do next weekend or maybe next month?

We are heading for summer - days are getting longer and surprise surprise the nights shorter.
I am still gainfully employed, still quite contented with my life in general and still not home-sick - only daughter-sick with Marinette and Michael in Cape Town.
Work is still "different" - even after twenty months. It takes some getting use to but I like this work/life balance policy that "they" employ (and enforce).

It is all rubbing off on me.
I am becoming an animal of habit or is that just old age silently creaking up?
Tend to do my washing on a Thursday, get up between 7:30 and 08:00 every morning Monday to Friday. That is if I am not sleeping over at that wee little town outside Belfast. Go to bed at about ten o'clock at night. Have oats and fresh fruit and coffee for breakfast during the week and an Irish Fry on weekends.

Eating out every Sunday at a pub somewhere in the country - found this place with the best Buffalo wings in the world; spicy with a real blue cheese dip.

Tea on Saturdays in the afternoon round about five where "tea" means a sit-down meal with a white table cloth and serviettes somewhere...

But back to work - Go for a lunch walk during the week to the local Sandwich bar or Centra for takeaways or Subway or Chinese (where you get big fat glorious potato chips with your Chinese). And the price - £7-00 for eat as much Chinese as you like - that includes a fortune cookie. Sandwiches vary from £2-99 to £4-50 with soup.

Weekends are really different - get up between 11 and 12 o'clock on Sundays and don't feel guilty about it: - no gardener to feed, to check on, to instruct in what to do and then to do it yourself. No car to wash, no pool to clean and we do have braais even though it is called BBQ's and 'they' know both how to 'braai' and how to 'down' things - be it food or drink.

Went to an Irish wedding last week Friday - lots to eat (and drink), good music and people.
People have no problem to call a cab to take them home. That is just the way that it is. If you drink then you don't drive. That and a few other civil things like letting cars in at crossings or allowing pedestrians to cross the road.

Anyway, enough of that for now. I must be sounding like a pain, but to be honest. I have no new news - a bit like Sky

News - just the same old story over and over and over. I can take up golf and bore everybody with that.

I am however thinking of the people back home.

Love to all.

View from my (Bready) upstairs guest bedroom...

Mirrored their way back, dropped in so to speak.
And that after I had the **wee** mirrors put up.

But some explanations first for those unfamiliar with potato speak.
'*Wee*' equates to 'tiny' or 'small' as in a *wee* cup of tea, my *wee* 22 stone 48 year old son still staying with me, the *wee* tractors that pull *wee* zillion litre tankers filled with *wee* loads of ponging liquid fertiliser all over the country to be sprayed where ever the air is smelling fresh and clean.

Interesting these tractors and a real pleasure to get stuck behind on your way to work as long as you don't breath. Tractors riding high on massive balloon tyres to get into the rain drenched fields. Asked a farmer the price of these tyres the other day. Round about £5000-00 if you replace all four on the tractor. I meant the price of the tyres on the trailer, he thought I meant the price of the tyres on the tractor - English, she is not spoken here.

But to wing back to my precious 'I-want I-want' swallows all the way from Sunny South Africa.
They are back, building their nests over the *wee* mirrors put up by the *wee* man that does not understand the meaning of *wee*.
The theory is that one puts up mirrors, *wee* mirrors in the spot where the swallows built their nests last time and then they wouldn't build there this time round as they were sort of

beaten to the roof, one could say. But these are no ordinary swallows, they are from Souf Africa and they like company, lots of company!
So now I am £90-00 poorer and a few families of swallows richer.

Not that I did not try to get them to shove off. I used my wee shaving mirror, a wee broom stick and leaning out of the upstairs main bedroom window, I knocked a nest down while looking into the mirror to find my way over my shoulder. And were they upset. Gave me a "*Eish Baas I am hungry Baas*", look and what could I do? I had to surrender. Once a Dutchman always a Dutchman as Tony would say.

Well the wee tiny small mirrors are about 6 by 8 inch light-shining-into-the-neigbours' eyes mirrors, so I guess the neigbours are quite pleased with the latest development. Nothing like swallow droppings to break a mirror's spirit. Don't forget the sun is up with the farmers at 4 and goes down after me at about eleven o'clock. And there was stupid old romantic me thinking that wee mirrors will bring back the days of the hippies - little round mirrors stuck onto long flowing flowery colourful dresses. There are lots of flowers in the fields and you should see my un-kept garden, overgrown with the most beautiful wee weeds, yellow flowers everywhere. It is a fertile smelling country.

I am keeping well. The credit crunch is squeezing my wallet but I guess everybody else is in the same boat.

I had a scan of the old liver and apart from very red, it seems to be fine. I am however still waiting for the official results.

70

I am scheduled to have a wee operation to have a "sunspot" removed from my forehead - quite a process in the land of National Health Services. I decided to go the NHS way even though the company provides private medical. Anyway, first one sees the GP, then the dermatologist (after waiting three weeks) for an autopsy, then you are booked for the operation etc etc etc. All correspondence via the Royal Mail Service. Everybody just assumes that letters will be delivered and that it will be delivered on time.

The weather on this wee island has been unbelievable over the last three plus weeks - lots and lots of sun with daytime temperatures in the middle to higher twenties - way too hot for me.

Weather is the only common language here. Everybody can speak weather and everybody is allowed to speak it: in the bank, the chemist, the shop, waiting rooms, work... Unlike criticising potatoes, only real Irishmen are allowed to give advice on potatoes.

Then, I am still gainfully employed even though the name of the company has changed to bring it more into the fold of the mother company in America - so it is no longer called Northbrook Technologies Northern Ireland but rather Allstate Northern Ireland.

Being employed I have to do some work now.

Take care and be good to yourselves.

PS My impersonation of Shrek - but then, I had ear ache.

So I am in the system - cut up so to speak.
The Brits and their rules and regulations - it is just not cricket.
No wonder the English Gentleman across the border has such a complex.

Anyway, I grew a horn.
Not the normal WAM thing. More like a *"rooi nek"* sun thing.
On my forehead: left as I look out. Right for those looking in.

Went to see the doctor that referred me to the dermatologist that referred me to the hospital where the horn was examined, touched and cooed over by a very attractive blond 27 year old unattached soft spoken left handed Irish girl with an educated accent. She was impressed by the good health that I am in generally and that my heart can beat faster and slower as she moved closer or further…

But, I still have my horn, even after it was examined by Mr. Stone-somebody - a surgeon.
Ja, I have to go for an operation that will be followed by skin craft (or is it graft?).
They are rushing it - my bed for the day booked for Tuesday the 15th of July 2008.

Not bad going - they work to NHS (National Health Service) rules. Rules that mean loads and loads of paperwork…
Everything explained to the detail that includes that it is normal that there will be blood, that stitches may have to be

73

removed at some later stage and that there may even be some pain. Even the expected level of discomfort that may be experienced - an hour of that and please sign here.

O Ja, and she (the very attractive blond unattached 27 year old left handed Irish Girl) also took a photo of my horn.
She assured me that I will not be recognizable from the photo.
The biopsy (not *autopsy* credit to Alan) returned a verdict of "*Squamous Cell Carcinoma*" with a good survival rate.
More to be disclosed, or is that uncovered / unearthed, during and after said operation.

We have also moved offices - Northbrook Technologies that are now known as Allstate Northern Ireland.
A bit more out of town and about two or three miles further away from my place of residence.
First occupants in the new building with dark wooden panelled toilets - the gents that is.
Business (work) has slowed down. Not that I or anybody else have been killing ourselves mind you.

The general work environment and conditions are under review at all times. I even volunteered and attended a full morning brain storming session on how-to-improve-the-all-important-work-life-balance.

We came up with 201 ideas that included wrist watches for everybody to run at American time, more holidays, more money, eye sight correction laser treatment, a coffee percolator that will have coffee on hand when one arrives at work and a whole lot more. Some ideas are already being implemented like working from home for up to two days a week - if your home work environment conforms to Health and Safety regulations - with a photo to prove. The company does not want to open itself up to claims.

Have fun.

Poor me!

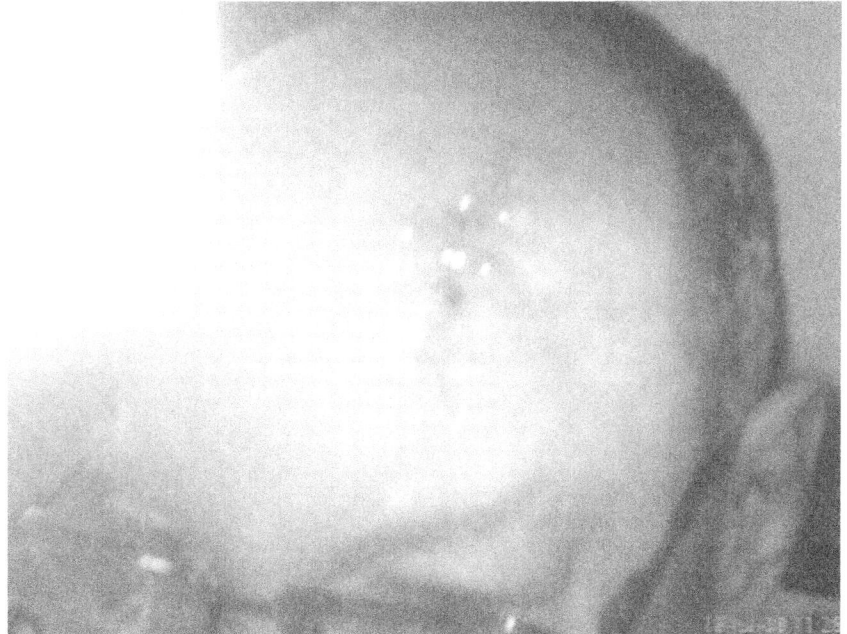

From: Johann Wentzel
Sent: 25 September 2008 18:28
23. Subject: My sentimental email (and I am only 56)

It was good, very good. I hope so for you too.

Seven thousand plus kilometres (some really really terrible squatter sheet teeth loosening gravel road - *I just did not want to listen*) later, twenty two days (one bad day weather-wise) by the calendar and we are back in friendly (weather & road-wise) Northern Ireland.

The flights were good - Airfrance & CityJet (we are a wee bit off the beaten track you know) - Dublin, Paris, JHB and JHB, Paris, Dublin - so the main hauler (Airfrance) planes were empty enough to allow us two seats each that translated into three for me and one for Linda: me being a bit taller.

Furthermore, an hourly bus runs 24/7 between Belfast and Dublin, but we got on and off at Banbridge; a few miles south of Linda's new house with spare bedrooms and clean linen centrally located at Waringstown.

Bottom line - we left O R Tambo at 19:45 on Tuesday evening and were home having a wee cup of tea before twelve yesterday (Wednesday) morning. With our bags this time, so no excuse for anyone.

It was good, very good - a place to unpack and settle, one wedding, one fiftieth birthday, one real braai, one new grandson-to-be scan, four of the Big Five and buckets of good memories - old ones dusted and new ones discovered.

It was a case of we came, we saw and we enjoyed and we will be back - me already in April.

I guess it will even get better with time and yes, it is a boy - Ty Stent or just maybe, just maybe Ty Michael David Stent!

It will be impossible to highlight any one moment or thank any one individual but here I go anyway:

Our base camp - out West Rand way.

The wedding - out of this world with the most beautiful bride ever (and I talk from experience).

The birthday party - I felt old! The birthday girl looked as if she could have been my daughter.

The braai - the South Africans know how to live.

The scan - what a miracle!

Even Cape Town and the drive down from Springbok - I can now understand certain things better, not that I will support their Rugby team, but M & M made a good move and we had a pleasant evening with Ronald and Aria at 93 (?) Winery Road.

It was good: good to see old friends, to see the country through different eyes, to smell and to taste.

It was especially good to share it with the Wild Irish Girl.

It was good to spend time with Freddie and Sonette, with Michael and Marinette, with people from The Bank, with Systems Advisers. Good to speak to Limont (even though he never replies to my emails) and to see Fritz and Hannah looking healthy.

Hoe kan ek dankie sê?
Vir Christo en Teena, vir Alta en Derek, vir Tony en Karen,

vir Freddie en Sonette, vir Michael en Marinette, vir Aria en Ronald!

Moet ook nie vir Florence en Anne vergeet nie, but it will not be fair to attempt to list all names.

It will however be unforgivable if I don't say thank you for genuine friendship, consideration & hospitality - having the wedding performed in English for the sake of the Irish visitor, for Tony and Karen for inviting the whole team over to their place. *Vir Freddie en Sonette vir hulle huis en gasvryheid, Derek en Alta (stuur fotos sodat ek weer kan kyk hoe regte hippies lyk), vir M & M...*

Enough of that for now.

I was impressed by how things have changed over the last two and a bit years!

Believe it or not: Service was good wherever we went.
Robben Island a real value-for-money experience even it nearly succeeded in making me feel bad for being a W A M, but that did not last long.

The view from Table Mountain was spectacular, the bush was good to us - lots and lots of buffalo, elephant, even a few crocs and hippos and only nine puncture holes on Linda's body that should eventually heal with not too much scarring - a wee reminder of the gemsbok park and the road via Vanzylsrus...

The roads were good (when I listened to advice) with lots of road works going on all over the country.

Also lots of buildings going up and we only had one power outage.

And things are definitely more expensive - a lot more. Not only petrol but eating out and the normal day to day things. The worse for prices were the so called duty free shops at the airport; the only place with bad customer service.

More to follow once I have been through the photos, have unpacked my case and have been through my post.

Regards,

From: Johann Wentzel
Sent: Thu 16/10/2008 15:48
24. Subject: I am and therefore I must be - still alive that is.

We are still in summertime here up North, but that will change in the next week or two, meaning that we will then be two hours behind South Africa. Also meaning that I would have been able to go 'home' if we were on SA time, but here I am killing myself with two hours to go.

The potato life is still good to me; even though I have had to cut down on my walking.
That was not by choice - not with the move of offices and the long and winding road from Londonderry/Derry via Newbuildings, Bready, Strabane, Sion Mills, Omagh, missing Dunnganon, hitting Lurgan through to Waringstown. That is, ignoring the little villages and pubs along the way.

Just over 80 miles of Northern Ireland road, constructed so as to not upset the Leprechauns and Fairies. In other words, built around big trees and the like: an old broken down tractor, an overgrown rose bush, crumbling stone walls... you know - things of real value.

Two hours plus of pure indulgence in green hills, white sheep, Jersey cows, rivers and mad Irishmen fly fishing in their strange waterproof longjohns worn over their normal layers of clothes. Fishing in the rivers, not their waterproofs; but wearing those rubber half bodies that drown those stupid enough to fish too deep and then not being able to surface when their pants fill with water and/or fish. Two hours of meditation while it rains, snows, suns shines and more rain but no dust, never. *O ja*, and crows / ravens and sometimes badgers, a strange white and black dog size animal with claws, splat over the black tar.

It really is a beautiful drive with lots of parking/picnic spots along the way. One can even take the alternate route - the scenic route, I kid you not! I have tried that: the scenic route on more than one occasion, but have got horribly lost (on more than one occasion). I am seriously thinking of getting a SATNAV - ABSA Account...

But back to the long and winding road - final destination Waringstown:

Lurgan and Waringstown merge as one with no clearly defined borders. Lurgan being the bigger of the two villages.

Lurgan also has a rail track running through the town with booms & bells that stop the afternoon traffic, a massive church bell/clock that accurately shows the time and lots of old grey buildings. I have on a few occasions confused the clock for the full moon on some of my earlier returns to Londonderry/Derry - the place that puts the food on the table and the petrol (now just under £1.10 a litre) in the car.

Waringstown (not to be confused with Warrington in England) is where Linda, the Wild Irish Girl, was born and where she still lives even though she works in a town called Ballymena.

She has been with the same company for over thirty years - first as a part timer whilst waiting to go to university. The company then offered her a scholarship (how can it be a scholarship if you go to university?) and then a position as a research scientist after qualifying, then as Team Leader on the factory floor and now as a Shift Manager - 300 people over two shifts. Poor thing works twelve hours shifts - 10 to 10 three days a week with a management meeting on day number 4. Except that she loves her job so much that she works 14 hour shifts!

Ballymena, County Antrim, is about 40 miles from Waringstown - an hour's drive via Moira and passing Belfast International Airport on the right (will be on the left on the way back).

Belfast has two international airports - Belfast International and Belfast City now called George Best after some guy that said that he spent his money on women and cars while he wasted the rest or something like that.

The "best" airport, and that is only my take on it, for international flights to and from South Africa, is still Dublin even though it is quite some way down towards the south and in the Republic of Ireland, BUT one misses Heathrow!!

For cheap across the Irish Sea hops there are Ryanair flying into Derry airport right next to the town of Londonderry/Derry or Easyjet flying into Belfast International or even flybe that uses Belfast City airport:
www.ryanair.com, www.easyjet.com, www.flybe.com.
One's choice will depend on where one would be departing from. If in doubt, www.ask.johann.wentzel!

Something else about this wee green Island.
Not only is it divided into North (UK with miles and Pounds & Pence) and South (The Republic of Ireland with kilometres

and Euros & Cents), but it is further carved into counties: Londonderry/Derry falls into County Londonderry, the village Bready where I live in Co Tyrone and Ballymena in co Antrim.

That all is the geography lesson for today, Thursday 16 October 2008.

Take care and be good to yourselves.

The Pretty One in front of her house in Waringstown!

If there is a world in every drop then what is Ireland?
Quite simple - the centre of the universe. The hair of the dog.
The trees are flaming different colours of autumn wetness and a clean white bed the magnet of one's existence.
But the sun still shines - not often but it does out there somewhere (I hope).

And I love it!

The weather, the colours, the fog blanket, the rain and the cold - it simply takes my breath away.
Especially on a Monday morning when I have to wheel the bin down the road - one week blue (paper-and-other-recyclables) the other week black (non-recyclables).
Why black I sometimes wonder, as the "binny" wheels splash through the shallow puddles?

It is about two hundred yards down the road to the central bin congregation point - 47 bins from our wee village not yet officially recognised even though there is a weekly rubbish collection service and even though we pay council tax (roughly £600-00 per annum) - still some town planning paperwork to be finalised and until such time ours is not to question why, ours is but to meet down the road to deliver.

It is autumn and life carries on even though the BBQ's have been put away. (I have not cleaned mine but it is stored safely in the wee sun-house behind the outside table inlayed with small tiles and the brown metal chairs, a wee mattress from last year's rollaway bed that was recycled, a strong plastic red checkered carry bag heavily filled with ocean washed coloured stoned from Marlin's Head and a few other odds and sods.)

Anyway, to get back to the weather and to centre of the universe:
People still turn up at work; the postman still does his thing with his little red truck as does the burner.
Most houses have an oil burner (supposed to be serviced once a year - £35 or there about) that: well burns oil that heats the house and feeds hot water to the geyser housed on the landing at the top of the stairs in the hot press. Nicely tucked away behind a normal sized wooden pine door.
Oil is currently £230-00 for 500 litres and I would say one may use about three to four times 500 litres per annum.
But that, like all things depends on whether children and wives realise that money does not grow on trees - too wet.
And that puts me in a very fortunate position - no money, no wives and no children. There must be some winter irony in that?
I am also on my second 500 litre delivery going into year two.

But I have a real fireplace at my wee semi-detached double storey house. I also think that some of my friendly neigbour's heat maintains or at least contributes, to the warm atmosphere in my house at Bready. The house with no money, wives or children and a double bed with an electric blanket.

My own bed linen is mainly white with a light orange to

brown thread woven into the one set that gets picked up by the earthly colours of my lined curtains that block the sun during the never ending summer month. I tend to only half dry the duvet- and pillow-covers before hanging it out over the upstairs doors to release the good clean fresh smell...

Anyway, Angela, the friendly lady next door (joined by a communal paper thin outside wall that is really a shared inside wall - remember it is two semi's) cooks and bakes much more than me and that also keeps the overall bigger "house" cozy. She does however not use a tumble dryer - too much electricity.

One can also heat the water in the geyser electrically - called *using-the-emersion* geyser and NOT *emergency* heater as I used to think. Never too old to learn.

Real people don't use the emersion geyser - don't really know why - may not be a real person, but I guess it must be because (coming from South Africa with the cheapest electricity in the world and 24 hours a day hot water on tap) I don't appreciate the cost difference between oil and electricity and the impact on the environment and my personal number nine carbon footprint.

I do however sometimes wonder whether it is better to heat everything in the house, both floors (all heaters all rooms) plus the geyser all at the same time or whether it is better to do it piece meal. Does it really save to turn the heaters in some rooms way down or even off? Is the heat rising from the ground floor not enough to maintain the heat upstairs? What is the answer to the purpose of life? Were we put here for a reason? Why does everybody worry about the credit crunch when we are indebted to and owned by The Banks anyway?

I do also sometimes forget to switch the burner off or the emersion geyser for that matter. The central heating has a timer but can be overwritten at will.
I also tend to use a wee old man's knee blanket when watching TV or to visit the friendly next door neigbour rather than burning oil.
Really no reason why the temperature must always be at a constant 23 degrees Celsius 24 hours of everyday.

The hot press? A wee little cupboard room where the geyser is and fitted with a few pine shelves to store towels, linen and the like.
The heat radiated by said geyser keeps the press, well hot.

All answers come to him that waits!
That is why men have all the wisdom.

Keep warm.

It is cold - Siberia cold.

It is wet - Northern Ireland wet.

And I will surely die, if my electricity should get cut; or if I should run out of oil; or if my wee Plum coloured two-door Ford Fiesta Zetec should break down on the ten mile trek to work; or if it should skid on the black ice and end up in the *mielie*-veld just outside Newbuildings. The *mielies* halfway between Bready with its 47 houses and Londonderry, the Walled City with its 100 000 or so citizens getting ready for Halloween this Friday the 31st of October 2008. Hundred thousand plus the 30 000 or so mainly Scottish tourists that cross the Irish Sea to come and have a good *craic*. It should be a field weekend for the 3000 plus registered taxis in our Walled City.

Ja, there is a farmer that has put his whole farm, must be all of 2,3 acres, put it all under *Vrystaat mielies*.

How is it possible that I can leave my desk for 15 minutes and come back to 11 work related emails? Don't people have better things to do?

It has also started sleeting - fat soft ice snowy rain drops fall from the grey sky that gives the atmosphere a spooky glow. Here I am sitting and working, warm in the comfort of being alive. I wonder whether the *mielies* will survive?

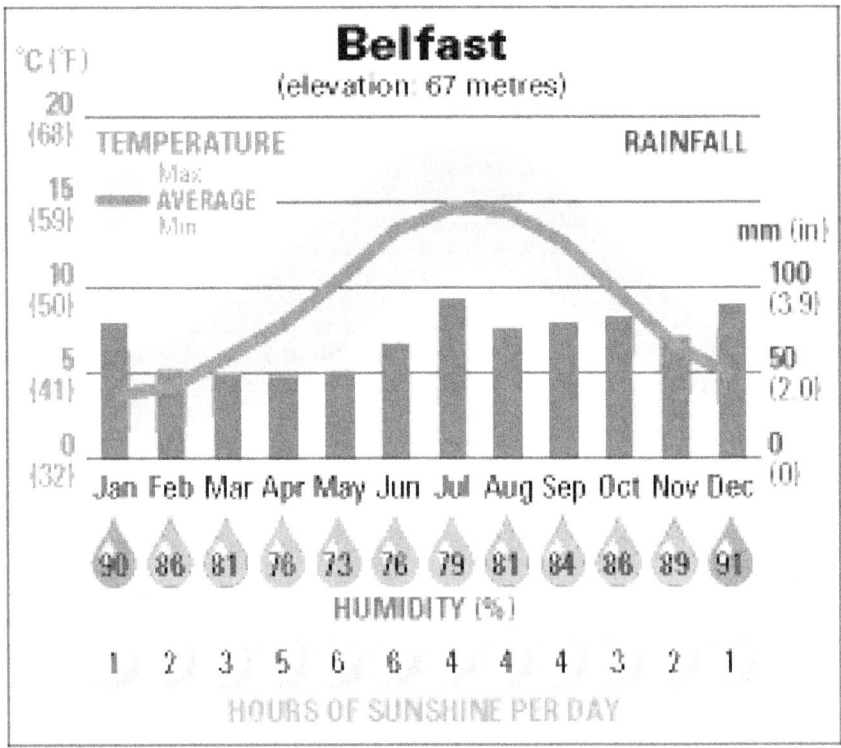

"There's probably no god, now stop worrying and enjoy your life" - http://www.justgiving.com/atheistbus

From: Johann Wentzel
Sent: Thu 30/10/2008 10:59
27. Subject: No news

Having a really beautiful nearly sunny day today - must be anything up to 9 degrees.

Not at work tomorrow - Friday the last day of October and also Halloween Day.
Going to Belfast to meet with somebody that is leaving for Canada - why?
The team that I am part of, Stat Interface is spread over two sites - Belfast and Londonderry / Derry.
Chris is from Belfast, in his middle twenties and is moving to Canada.
His mom passed away a few months ago - minutes after the family returned from Florida - deep vein thromboses due to the flight.
She was in her forties, a nursing sister, non-smoker, fit. Just shows.
Anyway, he decided it is time to spread his wings and went to Canada for a week to test the waters and the job market and now he is going.

I will also not be at work next Friday, the 7th of November.
Going to spend some time with Barry and Elbereth in Surrey - flying Friday afternoon and return Sunday afternoon. From/to Belfast International to/from London Gatwick. Total cost - nearly ninety pounds!! (real money). Would have been cheaper if I acted sooner.

Have a good weekend.

From: Johann Wentzel
Sent: Fri 14/11/2008 11:05
28. Subject: A song, a history lesson and some personal news

Oh Danny boy, the pipes, the pipes are calling
From glen to glen, and down the mountain side
The summer's gone, and all the flowers are dying
'Tis you, 'tis you must go and I must bide.
But come ye back when summer's in the meadow
Or when the valley's hushed and white with snow
'Tis I'll be here in sunshine or in shadow
Oh Danny boy, oh Danny boy, I love you so.
And if you come, when all the flowers are dying
And I am dead, as dead I well may be
You'll come and find the place where I am lying
And kneel and say an "Ave" there for me.
And I shall hear, tho' soft you tread above me
And all my dreams will warm and sweeter be
If you'll not fail to tell me that you love me
I'll simply sleep in peace until you come to me.
I'll simply sleep in peace until you come to me.

Danny Boy is a song whose lyrics are set to the old Irish tune Londonderry Air and here is today's history lesson now that we have covered the cultural side:

None of this is my own words of course!

Londonderry and Derry refer to the same place, a city in the north of Ireland, and also to the surrounding county. Supposedly the city of Derry was founded by St. Colmcille, although archaeological evidence shows that people were living there thousands of years earlier. There is an excellent museum in the city, which is worth a visit if you want to find out more. The name of the city was actually "Doire", corrupted to "Derry" by people who can't pronounce Irish. It thought to derive from an Irish root meaning "oak tree"

Moving quickly along in history, about a millennium later the government of England was having a difficult time colonizing Ireland because of the fierce and warlike clans living there, especially in the north of the country, Ulster. The monarchs of England, almost all of whom were notorious cheapskates, were continually looking about for ingenious ways to conquer places without actually having to put up the money themselves, or run the risk of unpopularity if they lost. In the case of Ireland, some of these schemes of the "Brish gummit" (as it is termed nowadays in Ulster) are still producing unfortunate long-term consequences.

In 1608, King James I gave the city of Derry to the City of London corporation. I guess the deal could be summed up by saying that if the City of London could figure out a way to chase all the inhabitants out of Derry, they would be allowed to keep the loot, minus a percentage for the King of course. If they lost, well too bad. In celebration of this historic agreement, the name of Derry was officially changed to Londonderry. (For further information, check out the Northern Ireland Tourist Board's _History of Derry_.)

The linguistic outcome of all this today is that, if you think that King James's deal with the City of London was a good idea, you call both the city and county "Londonderry". If you do, you are probably a supporter of the Unionist movement that seeks to keep Ulster a part of the United Kingdom. If you think it was a bad idea, you call both "Derry", and you are probably a supporter of the Irish Nationalist cause. Or you might just be someone who thinks it's confusing for kings to be going around changing the

94

names of places all the time for no good reason.

You can find plenty of discussion about the political side of the question elsewhere, but here let's look at the musical side. We have an air, collected in county Derry / Londonderry, and it doesn't have a title. What do we call it?

If you were a proper Victorian, there's no way you were going to call it the Londonderry Air, much less the Derry Air, because of the improper sentiments that these titles might suggest. My parents tell me that in their youth in Australia, it was usually called the Air from County Derry. (This would, I suppose, support Winston Churchill's theory that Australia was inhabited by "convicts and Irishmen".)

And there I was thinking that Australia is still only inhabited by convicts.

Anyway on a more personal note after this somewhat long introduction:

My son Werner, is not well. So much so that we were told that he may not make it for much longer and that we should hope that it will be earlier rather than later as he is in some pain and struggling. This has been going on for some time with the real turning point over the last week or three leading into Monday when Anne-Marie was once again called by the nursing staff at Vita Nova, Daggafontein, Springs. I have also been in contact with them, but that is not so easy as they are quite reluctant to commit over the phone - what I can understand.

I must however be honest that he was already in bad shape when Linda and I were in South Africa in September.

Anne-Marie has been spending time with him and I will fly out when we know what is going for what. It is difficult to quantify these things, but we were told that it may drag on for three months or even longer...

He seems to have lost interest and wants to spend time in his bed - this is a problem as he may suffocate 'drown' as his lungs and other organs are under stress. His fingers are swollen and he seems to be "peeing" all the time, complaining about pains in his legs and his head.

He will also be 34 on the 20th of this month. It was (is) quite an emotional time for Anne-Marie, Elbereth, Marinette and myself plus obviously those people that share our lives with us - Michael, Barry, Linda, our brothers, sisters and others.

We were asked about life support systems, but have indicated that we would prefer him not to be put on any unnecessary support systems when the time comes.

Elbereth is flying out next Thursday to spend some time with Anne-Marie and with Marinette. Anne-Marie unfortunately taking the major responsibility.

Fluit fluit my storie is uit - for now anyway.

From: Johann Wentzel
Sent: Mon 15/12/2008 14:11
29. Subject: Bready NT82 0EQ

Slip sliding to work
   and back
  and to work
   and back
and …
… so it goes…
… five mornings (in the dark) and five afternoons (in the dark) a week.
And then the long slide to/from Waringstown every Friday afternoon immediately after work and every Monday morning immediately before work.

No sun, no moon, no star … just lots & lots of cold white icy stuff (that becomes a problem when it turns black) and a salty spray that dirties the cars.
I even had to physically scrape the ice off my car last week Thursday afternoon at half past five, before sliding for home.
That is normally an activity reserved only for the mornings and then only if it isn't raining.
Rain means it is not cold enough for ice/frost to form on the cars.
But I am from Africa - clever - so I park as close to the wall as possible and only have to scrape half a car some mornings, depending on the rain…
It is also possible to start your car, go back into the house for a cup of coffee - no hijackers in wait, must be too cold.

It is beautiful and nice and all-embracing: the cold fresh air, the drive to work and then the drive back to a warm cozy

97

wee house and even warmer cozier double bed with electric blanket, a pile of easy-to-read books and lots & lots of Quality Street chocolates (two X 1.2 kg tins for £9.00) and KP honey roasted peanuts (£2.75 a tin).

The local farmers are contracted to spray the roads with a mixture of salt and a fine gravel when there is ice on the way.
This leaves the milky white deposit on the cars and is a bit of a problem when the windscreen washer is all frozen up - a bit like insects on the windscreen when travelling through the Karoo, just very different. Most of the salt cum gravel is mined just outside Belfast - half a million tonnes of de-icing rock salt per annum - just Google *Salt Mining in Northern Ireland* - very interesting.
It also sounds as if your car is being sandblasted when you pass the sprayers - like the road to Lüderitz though the desert when the wind blows.

The sun (if there is a sun) only rises after eight (long after) in the mornings and sets before 4 in the afternoons and then it is dark!
Dark with lots & lots of soft Christmas lights: Blue pin point firefly lights buzzing over the trees, bigger red ones snaking up and down the lampposts and all colours of the rainbow blinking at every house, inside and out with white and red stop signs shouting "*Santa please stop here*" - one sign for every child in the house (and a few adults I guess).

It really is invitingly colourful with Santas standing in full flight in the upstairs landing looking for naughty children, Christmas trees with lots & lots of lights - lights like jelly tots. And lots & lots of chocolates.

We had a pig scare - contaminated ham, bacon, joints, roasts - all pork products bought since the 1st of September had to be thrown away - EU rules and regulations. TG I am from Africa, so I could eat my honey cured roasted ham - £7.00 for 0,4 kg at ASDA. The smell - out of this world! The taste - to die for!!

But, pork is back on the shop shelves and the world is kosher/halaal again and Christmas on its way. The sun will make its turn and will come back.

But first we will have a sit-down Christmas meal of ham and turkey with lots & lots of stuffings and green & yellow vegetables and potato (lots & lots) and heavy Christmas pudding with brandy sauce and then lots & lots of chocolates.

Have a good one.

Lurgan Castle also known as Brownlow House:

Lurgan borders Waringstown (or it may be the village of Waringstown bordering Lurgan) and this was when the Lurgan lake was frozen solid.

Here I am, sandwiched at work between holiday and holiday; earning my Christmas pud in the sweat of my brow and it is cold - the weather, not the pudding.

It was all white this morning (still white at 12 o'clock when we went out to get something to eat) and there I was thinking that it may be snow, but even that was not to be - it was (is) ice: frost and minus 5 degrees. It is however dry and it is so beautiful with even colder weather predicted for the rest of the week and the weekend and tonight is Monday, so it must be pizzas with my friendly neigbour!

There are no hungry people in Northern Ireland and that is a fact. Isn't that unbelievable?

I was listening to a talk on the radio on the 24th of December 2008 and that was when it was mentioned - nobody in Northern Ireland will go hungry on Christmas Day for a lack of food!

And, I must be honest - I was eating for all the hungry children in Africa! Melon and orange followed by turkey and ham and three different types of stuffing and vegetables and salads and Marks & Spencer's cheesecake and ice-cream with a whole Christmas pudding still waiting, even after 4 days - I just could not. Even I from Africa had to admit defeat. Not even the red wine and Bailey's could wash it down and create just that wee empty spot for the Christmas pudding and rich Brandy flavoured custard.

To be quite honest - It is actually too much and a lot of food must go to waste if not to waist!

This first world culture, even in a credit crunch, is not healthy with too easy access to far too much with no real appreciation of what it may be to go without. It is like eating Nightingale tongues because that is just the thing to do and everybody is quick to blame the government if the singing should dry up - horror forbid. Not a case of seek and you shall find, more a case of blame and you will be given to stuff your face and shut you up.

There will be a special once-off payment to old age pensioners and certain others of £150.00 this month - this is only in Northern Ireland and then another £60-00 in January from the government for all pensioners in the UK (that includes Northern Ireland). This is intended to ensure that they don't go cold.

And we are all encouraged to spend the country out of recession; people queued from 5 in the cold for the bargains of Boxing Day...

Anyway, all that I wanted to say was, have a great 2009 and may all your needs be satisfied and may you never go hungry (or cold).

From: Johann Wentzel
Sent: Fri 13/02/2009 15:59
31. Subject: Friday the 13th and an hour to go!

To go home that is.
Waringstown home that is!

Surprise surprise the sun was shining earlier today. That is after the snow and rain of the last few days and litres and litres of oil burned to keep my wee home (that is Bready) warm and cozy.

But, they (the government I guess) are planning a new road from Dublin/Omagh via Strabane and Bready to L'Derry and it may just go right over my wee semi-detached double storey house - that is if I am lucky. I can't however see them (the government in consultation with the people) come to any agreement, never mind starting on the road for at least another three to four years. Everybody and I mean everybody can make suggestions, disagree, cry, write to the papers, object, bribe before the road will even be marked out.

I personally think that the road will follow the Foyle River when it gets to Bready. I will support that! Will make it easier to get to work and to get home - that is Waringstown home and where I will be spending Valentine's Day tomorrow.

Did you know Saint Valentine is the patron saint of bee keepers and of greeting card manufacturers as well? He is quite a busy man, or is that saint? He also protects travellers and happy marriages (not too successfully sometimes I would say) and then the patron saint of love...

103

Things are going well in Northern Ireland with or without the saint's help, how will I ever know whether he had a hand or bee sting in it? But then, my youngest Marinette's baby Ty is due any day, hour, minute and I believe Michael is standing ready with the camera!

Exciting indeed and maybe I should thank said saint for that. They are the best couple ever and I can only hope and pray that their son will take after them, sort of skipping the previous generation. Wish I was there but I should be flying out on the 12th of May for a first introduction. First giving said couple, mother-in-law, mother and sister their change.

Have a lovely Valentine's Day.

From: Johann Wentzel
Sent: Tue 17/02/2009 16:23
32. **Subject:** *Ty is gebore en ek wil skoon flou word!*

Was op die ou end 'n keisersnee want hy was blykbaar bietjie groot vir Marinette.

Sy is heel emosioneel a la Michael - wou 'n normale gebootre gehad het maar dokter het gesê genoeg is genoeg.

Het nog nie eers gewig of ander inligting nie maar alles het goed afgeloop en natuurlik is hy pragtig en al klaar die slimste kleintjie ooit!

From: Johann Wentzel
Sent: Tue 17/02/2009 16:32
33. Subject: So my first grandchild (grandson) was born a few minutes ago.

Still waiting for detail but he will be named Ty (don't ask me where the name came from but that was Marinette's choice) surname Stent, Ty Michael Stent.

Was a caesarean in the end and she is quite emotional as she wanted a normal birth.

Watch this space for further detail re weight, photos, etc of the brightest child ever!

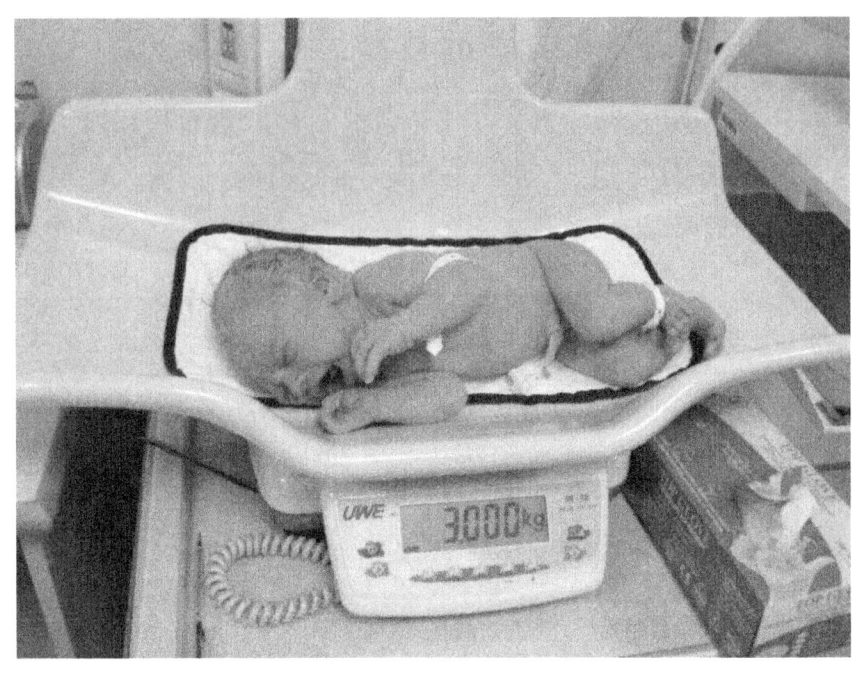

From: Johann Wentzel
Sent: Tue 24/02/2009 16:53
34. Subject: Summer has sprung! Temperatures are into double digits (well nearly)

And the sun shines (well nearly).
All jokes aside, the weather is mild with the midday temperatures up to 11, 12 even 13: cloudy most of the time and wet - this is Ireland you know. The Emerald Isle no less and lots and lots of nice fresh Queens, Pinks and Roosters (potatoes for the uneducated)!

Elbereth was here last weekend - arrived late Friday and departed late Sunday.

We (Adam (Linda's son), Linda, Elbereth (my daughter and since the 17th of February 2009 an aunt) and yours truly) had a good time, a visit to The Spur in Belfast on Saturday for spicy chicken wings, crumbed mushrooms, steaks, milkshake, dom pedro...They even stock Castle (but we stayed away from that - too many chemicals). But we had a potato with sour cream and chips. The total bill for four - a few pence short of £85-00.

Then Sunday was a home cooked meal by Linda followed by Lemon Maringa a la Elbereth's family recipe. And what did the clever child ask?
"*What is this on my plate*" - did not expect to see two potatoes dishes - this is Ireland you know! But she finished it! Both the mash and the wee little tasty oven grilled round sausage shaped potato thingies!
It was a good meal!!
With good company.

107

And a good weekend flowing into a good week.
So life is good - this is Ireland…

And this is the man!

Take care,

So Saint Patrick's Day came and went and there are still no snakes in Ireland.
For information on fleas please read Frank McCourt's novel *"Angela's Ashes"*. It is all the fault of the English, as are many other things, not only fleas.

The sun is shining. It is really warm, I joke not, but back to St Patrick's Day.
I did do my bit for St Patrick's Day - I mowed the lawn (Linda's) and that should count - grass is green. It is still greener this side of the fence, I joke not!

The Irish, irrespective of religion, all had a good Saint Patrick's Day followed by breakfast at work this morning - eggs, bacon, juice, coffee, beans, toast. Good oily stuff to line the old stomach.
But the grass is still green on this side of the ocean. Work is tapering off a wee bit (must we worry?), the days are getting longer and we will be moving into summer time at the end of March.

Did you know that this results in a 5% increase in heart attacks? Heart attacks also decreases by 5% when we move into winter time. Apparently all to do with lack of sleep and that we humans now (21st century) make do with the minimum hours of sleep ever. In other words, skipping just one hour of sleep pushes up the rate of heart attacks as we should have at least 7,5 hours of peaceful sleep per night to stay healthy, wealthy and wise.

Furthermore, you should be taking 100 steps each minute for half an hour a day if you want to achieve 'moderate' exercise by walking, but don't despair there is hope. People who are overweight or obese - which is the majority of middle to older adults (i.e. all my friends) - are working harder in order to carry their weight for any walking speed. They will need to downgrade their speed accordingly. The full study is available, at a small fee to be deposited into my South African ABSA account for those interested in living to a ripe old age.

Living to a ripe old age as long as you are not a British soldier in Northern Ireland.
We (Linda, her Mom, her Dad and I) went to the Massereene Army Barracks in Antrim where the two British soldiers were shot and killed by the Real Irish Republican Army eight or so days ago. I had to go and leave some flowers with an Afrikaans message - *Rus in Vrede*. Another two soldiers and a pizza delivery guy were also wounded in the attack.

Come to think of it, being a police officer in Northern Ireland may also be a problem. A police officer of the PSNI was murdered by dissident republicans in County Armagh in a place called Craigavon. That is more or less on Linda's doorstep. PSNI stands for Police Service Northern Ireland.

I could have been back in sunny South Africa. It is really hot today.

First read the book before watching the DVD - *Angela's Ashes*. It reminded me of my days as a child in "*Suid-Wes Afrika*".

From: Johann Wentzel
Sent: Thu 16/04/2009 09:28
36. Subject: Spring has sprung - again

I must be getting old, have taken to dosing in front of the TV with the fire going. Can do this for hours on end - sort of meditating and solving humankind's problems: the credit crunch, the never ending chase for material things, Michael Jackson's troubles, life after death, women and babies... important things.

Where was I again? Oh yes, it must be Spring. There was no ice on my car the last few days and people are cutting grass. Real people cutting grass and the temperature shooting up to 12 or 13 degrees some days. We even went for a picnic last Sunday. Picnic at Newcastle Northern Ireland. Really pretty town with a walkway winding on for miles and miles next to the ocean.

The town, Newcastle Northern Ireland, is at the foot of Slieve Donard, the highest mountain peak in Northern Ireland and part of the Mourne Mountain. And it was cold. Our wee wooden picnic table and benches on the well maintained lawn next to the winding walkway had no protection and the wind was pushing in from the ocean. The two old people - Linda's parents (Dad 85 in Nov, Mom 79 in a month or so) were laughing wet with red cheeks and out of breath due to the cold air. It was really good fun, them two old people cozy back in the car and Linda and I finishing the hot tomato soup and sandwiches (salmon and prawns). Life is great in Northern Ireland even though we have to cut our own grass, do our own washing and ironing, cleaning, cooking, etc. Cars can be washed (outside only) for £4-00 or

£5-00 depending on where you go. It is real people washing the cars. Their poor hands, red form the cold.

My new condensed working arrangement has its pros and cons. My 4-day work week makes my actual work day quite long. I try to be at work anywhere between 07:30 and 08:00 and leave the office round about 6 o'clock at night. The sun only sets well after 9 o'clock - it is Spring you know.

Anyway, where was I? Oh yes, I get to work somewhere around 07:30, switch on my PC, go and have my oats (social club supplies the milk and work supplied the industrial sized Microwave) and tea (Rooibos that I have to buy myself), fill my water bottle with cold water, get back to my desk and check my emails. Lots and lots of emails as we are well ahead of the States - not the Free State that killed the Sharks!

Anyway, there are always millions of emails due to the time difference, but there are also about five hours to reply before the States wake up. Why did it take the Cheetahs so long to wake up?

Where was I? Oh yes, Slieve Donard (or *Sliabh Dõnairt* in Irish) is in the province of Ulster, (Ulster with its formidable Rugby team) and is 849 meters high. It is on the east coast (that means Newcastle is on the east coast of Northern Ireland and not in the Free State). By the way, the highest mountain in Ireland is Carrauntoohil. Why they would call it a 'hill' when it is a mountain I don't know, but then this is Ireland.

All these things I meditate about while staring deep into the flickering fireplace at Linda's place while she does the ironing and the cooking and the cleaning. But come and visit and see for yourself. Northern Ireland is a green heaven on earth.

Take good care and sleep warm. It must be getting cold in Sunny South Africa.

Slieve Donard:

PS - Slieve Donard is named after Saint Domangart, also known as Saint Donard.

There is a koppie stone wall that criss-crosses the shoulders of the mountain, called the Mourne Wall, don't ask me why. This part of Northern Ireland also known as the province of Ulster. Ulster is made up of the six counties that is Northern Ireland plus Donegal, Cavan and Monaghan. Don't ask me why they not just call Northern Ireland Ulster. I just know (but I may be wrong) that if you play Rugby for "Northern Ireland" then you play for Ulster.

113

If you make the combined Ireland team then you play in a green jersey for, surprise surprise, Ireland. Ulster (Northern Ireland) has a flag showing a red hand against a white background, the bloody hand of Ulster or something like that. The koppie stone walls in Ireland are real works of art packed over centuries by real people.

There are really lots to mediate about in Ulster.

Road to nowhere...

What a long weekend - four days of Sun & Sea...

Temperatures in the twenties, company the best, the food excellent and the ocean unbelievable.
(It was actually 17 degrees at seven o'clock on Sunday evening and remember - the sun only sets after nine at night!)

To start where all stories should start: "Once upon a time long long ago in a distant land... just across the border there is a place called Ballyliffin".

So we went to Ballyliffin on Saturday.
But we first went to Letterkenny on Friday evening to spend time with Andrew and Annette.
Both Letterkenny and Ballyliffin are in ROI - the Republic of Ireland and the four pizzas came from Pat's Pizza at 9 Market in Letterkenny.
The chocolate cake and the apple tart were home baked and what a baker. Andrew has made a good catch!

This story however is not about Andrew & Annette or the Pizza's or the cakes or even about Letterkenny even though Letterkenny a la Ronald & Aria had a major influence in my original decision to trek to Ireland all those many moons ago.

It is rather about Ballyliffin and the rock, an island (not an Afrikaner), in the middle of the bay - Pollan bay. Ballyliffin's bay is called Pollan Bay and the rock (sorry island) is called Glashedy.

Interesting the local names, isn't it, but trust the English to spoil everything with their translations. Glashedy is The Green Cloak Island in English or something like that. I guess it will be called "*die Groen Gras Eiland*" once Zuma has liberated the world!

Ballyliffin is "down south" in County Donegal.

I can not take credit for the photos!

The weather was fantastic and the ocean view unbelievable. I must admit the water was tweezer cold but then we did not go to swim but to walk.

That must be the best about this island (Ireland), being so off the beaten track. There are always very few people wherever you go, clean white beaches and this time round, lots of sun. The weather plays a big big part in life in this part of the world. All you need is a few minutes of sunshine and everything looks up.

We have friends, Peter and Caroline with a holiday home high on the hill overlooking Ballyliffin, Pollan Bay and Glashedy, the "green rock" and they invited us for a meal at the local Ballyliffin hotel to celebrate Linda's fiftieth birthday. What a meal: seafood chowder, medium rare aged fillet, yogurt dessert, wine, coffee, cheese and sides of potato - chilly, garlic, chips. A feast for a king at the hotel below!

May the sun be good to you until next time.

It is warm, hot, cooking. Too hot for my liking and the end is not in sight! Clouds and possible cooling rain only predicted towards the end of the week!

The sun is blazing down on my poor wee head from 4 in the morning till 11 at night and I kid you not. It floods the rooms, the hallways, my car and there is no place to hide. It is hot and the sun is bright and the Irish girls are saving on cloth, bursting out all over ones face and my glasses are all steamed up - TG for dark glasses.

As I stated before - it must be the rich creamy white Irish milk - they know how to overflow. But 'it' is changing from milk white to a sore red. ... Saying should have been *"Irish and mad dogs"*...

Warning: Do not believe the temperatures shown by Sky TV. It is much much higher in real skin life. So much for climate change - it is going to kill me. The heat is forcing me to 'work' from 07:30 in the morning to 18:30 at night and there is no way that I am putting a hair outside at lunch time. My curtains and blinds are permanently drawn, the grass goes uncut and I even went for an indoor swim at the Lurgan public pool - £3.20. There were just about no people in the pool, only two lifeguards bored to tears on their high chairs. The pool water was lukewarm and the deep end was 13' 0". No diving allowed. I wonder how they manage to varnish the wooden ceiling hundred of yards above the pool. It must be a Health and Safety nightmare.

And are the Boks only going to kill the British & Irish Lions! Can't wait to see the pharmacist's face after the first test on the 24th of June. Johnny, the pharmacist is a big rugby follower as is Peter the dentist that I went to see this morning. Broke a tooth while in South Africa. Peter, the dentist is very politically correct - said I have a *complicated bite*! Complicated bite but that it is still good for a number of years - image me with dentures!

He, Peter has a brother with a place somewhere on the Garden Route. The accents still floor me at times when they curl around the Sound African place names so I don't know exactly where - could have been Knysna but could also have been Umtata or even Sedgefield. Sedgefiled where Marinette planted her feet, her hands in her sides and declared: "I *am not staying in this house. The wolf will blow it down.*" That was 25 years ago and there she is now, the mother of the most beautiful boy in the world. The Irish sun will also fry his head, he takes after me.

I, for the first time, noticed all the SA accents on the Cape Town radio station while entertaining Ty - why do Afrikaners speak English when talking to one another?

Anyway, life is still treating me well even though it is hot. I am still privileged to work a four day week with a three day weekend. That is except for every eight weeks when I have a four day weekend - that is when I change from Friday off to Monday off. All weekends are spent away from the walled city of Londonderry and I am seriously thinking of putting my house up for rent. That will mean that I will have to relocate offices to Belfast. I am a bit reluctant as I really don't want to overstress the relationship but I guess time will tell / force

120

my not too reluctant hand. We, Linda and I, have already booked our tickets for the next trip to South Africa at the end of September - Air France *nogal*! The idea is to spend some time with Michael, Marinette and Ty in Cape Town and then to work our way up to Durban / Ballito via East London, Knysna, PE, Addo Elephant Park, etc. Then to cut across to JHB to visit Werner, brother Freddie and his wife Sonette and to catch the plane back to good old Dublin.

O ja, and we are going to Switzerland at the end of August - for my birthday on the 24th. All birthday presents may be posted / shipped / delivered to Waringstown. Deposits into the ABSA account as per previous years will be greatly appreciated. I will be 57 on the 24th of August 2009. The 25th of August was the day that I first communicated with Linda. That was nearly two years ago.

Back to Switzerland. Friends have an apartment and a yacht next to and on the lake and have invited us to join them. This time we accepted and have already booked the tickets - Easyjet. I don't need a visa for Switzerland so that makes it a wee bit easier. I also don't require a visa for Turkey *Istanbul so that is there somewhere on the horizon.

Work is not too stressful and I am at times concerned about the possible impact of the credit crunch on actual work coming in. Guess that is a worldwide issue and I shouldn't worry. It is however in my nature to sometimes worry. Gives me a purpose.

Talk about worry - I had an interesting experience at Heathrow terminal 4 when I came back from South Africa. They, the Brits at customs did not realise that I have been in the country since July 2006 as I originally entered via Dublin on that day nearly three years ago. This is in spite of me paying my UK taxes like a good citizen, having a national insurance number, using the national health service (that is excellent), having contacted the UK Home Office on more than one occasion, surrendered my South African driver's license for an UK one, etc etc etc. But all ended well and I was allowed to make my way back to Northern Ireland. Don't know what will happen when I have to renew my visa or apply for 'Indefinite Leave to Remain'. I still have two years to go (I hope) before I have to worry about that.

And I am voting on Thursday. We are voting for the EU parliament. Northern Ireland has three members representing us.

Take good care and don't forget the sunblock.

From: Johann Wentzel
Sent: Tue 16/06/2009 14:09
39. Subject: RE: Greetings from South Africa

David.
Slaan my om met 'n nat vis!

Well, good luck and it can only be an adventure!
Quite an adjustment I must admit and it will be up to you to keep the family sane. (I think it is easier for us men... so stay positive).

Don't forget to pack a few good old SA CD's, things that you will never listen to at home. Makes for fun when you have a braai and listen to it here in the new country.

There was a program on BBC - Billy Connelly touring good old England, Ireland and even Wales (it is available from Amazon) and I enjoyed watching it (even though he does use the "f" word a bit too much to my liking) and have decided to tour a bit more - really is a beautiful small country (can cover most of it in a few days).

As far as **dress code** - you will be 100%. I have not worn a tie or suit for work since I started here. No jeans, just long sleeve shirts and smart pants or trousers as it is referred to here.

We do have a dress-down day on Fridays when jeans are allowed but no rugby tops, etc - all to do with being politically correct and not offending anybody. I have worn a suit to a wedding and to a funeral - be warned they dress up for "special" occasions. I was underdressed at the funeral!

123

I still maintain my bank account (ABSA) in SA and have had no problems transferring money into it or drawing from it. My local account is with Barclays International (offshore) and was opened for me by ABSA. It was a slight problem as there are no Barclays branches in Ireland so I have to post cheques to be deposited to the "Main Land". I also kept on working from here for sometime - and kept on putting in my normal SA tax return. I am now submitting a null return.

I did ask the local company's pension adviser about the potential future impact of any possible funds or income from SA re my situation and her reply was "what they don't know will not hurt them - why don't I not just use that money when visiting SA?", was her question, but I will rather play it safe. I also had a letter from Barclays after my first year to clarify my situation re tax on my savings and is having tax deducted from that as per any local.

I have found that using my SA credit card costs more than drawing money from my SA current account - the credit card attracts an international fee while my bank card does not - the exchange rate also seems to be better.

A few other pointers (and I may add more later if I think of anything).
Good idea to get proof of any no claim bonuses from your short term insurer. It made quite a difference for me with both my car and house content insurance.
Then, if possible an unabridged copy of your wedding certificate. A normal wedding certificate is no good in Northern Ireland.

A few certified copies of important documents - passport,

wedding certificate, SA ID (I had to send certified copies of that back to SA on a few occasions!), etc.

Then I had to surrender my SA driver's license to get a UK one - I also had a one year international driver's license from the AA that was good enough to hire a car in Northern Ireland.

It is also good to open an account ASAP when you get here - just to build up some sort of credit reference. I subscripted to SKY TV and they offered me a credit card after a few months that I took up.

Lastly, I also had my name added to the voter's role - can be done after three months up north - don't know about your side of the border.

Then, get your dad to join a senior club (centre) once you have settled. My lady friend's mother attends one three times a week - they collect and drop her, feed her for £1-30 a day and she loves it.

Finally - don't forget to let the SABC know that you have left the country else they will demand payment for your TV license!

And that is about all - give it a chance and you are going to have a good time.

Or then the new Wimbledon retractable roof or the rain that fell on the mad 36,500 revellers that descended on Stonehenge on the longest day of the year - the summer solstice. Longest day for us up here if not for those down there at the south point of darkest Africa. Strange how those that want to save the planet can leave such a lot of rubbish behind but then Stonehenge is on the Salisbury Plain and we all know what happened to Salisbury.

© SIMON CHAPMAN/PIN

The sun is ruining it, my life that is unlike those lives ruined by the so-called financial fraud of Madoff. How can losing money ruin lives? Does that mean that people, (99% of the world's population) without money to invest in pyramid schemes all have ruined lives? Did he not take money only by invitation from the rich and famous personally referred? Did most not receive returns on their investments in the good times? Those same rich and famous that exploited not only others but have ruined mother earth to the extend that it is up to the misguided not-thinking-for-themselves ruined 99% to now live green in an attempt to keep them rick folk in the luxuries that they have not earned?

Anyway, be it as it may, it is due to them the exploiters (if I have to believe the doom prophets and I definitely don't but that is another story), that caused the 30+ degree Celsius never ending days of no-where-to-hide-from sun that I now have to endure. Remember the sun rises at 4 and sets after 10 at night - 16 hours of sticky heat under a blistering British sun if not empire. Also remember, the sun sets later here where I am earning my bread in the sweat of my brow, that is the case across the sea and down in London.

Strange lot, them the English, now that Andrew Murray may win Wimbledon and it is still a big "may" in my books after last night on centre court under the Wimbledon Roof. Strange that they, the English, now call him one of their own - the first Englishman in many years (something like 74 years or so) to win Wimbledon. But he is not, he is Scottish. Anyway, the Irish got it their way - it is the British & Irish Lions touring Souf Africa. Not the British Lions.

What an assh*le Schalk Burger! I also watched that epic movie Zulu, made in 1964 this weekend. I wonder how much they paid them Zulu impis. Not enough to have left them with the need to invest the money for the sake of money. Money, to them the "plain stupid" ones, was the means not the goal. How much we have to learn, how little time.

I have been at work since 07:15 this morning - the first day of my four day week and TG the aircon is working: stuff the impact that this is having on climate change. I live in a first world society that craves immediate satisfaction, now. A throw away society where we have to spend at an ever increasing frenzy to oil the wheels of prosperity. Talking about ruined lives.

Take good care - the word is out! BAB (bonuses are back - for bankers at least). A funny lot the Brits.

So sheep are growing smaller because of climate change, but it is actually more than that.

It is only wild sheep on some Scottish island and they are not really shrinking.

It is just that because of the shorter winter the weaker and smaller sheep don't die, but survive.

Something like 5% sheep shrinkage over the last 25 years.

All this "*because survival conditions are not so challenging - even the slower growing sheep have a chance of making it, and this means smaller individuals are becoming increasingly prevalent in the population*".

Replace "**smaller**" by "**stupider**" - makes you think...

Sort of proof of the origin of sheep, I guess.

Have always known that by not killing off the weak we have diluted the gene pool.

Where will it end?

Giving the right to have children to couples of the same sex, the vote to females, allowing anybody to drive a car on a public road, the young mum effect, free medication for self inflicted conditions, believing that going green and paying more taxes will save earth?

Should never have allowed vegetarians and the like to breed.

Have a good weekend and may Schalk Burger never play Rugby again.

131

The background detail for the older generation - those with an attention span of more than 30 seconds:
Climate change is causing a breed of wild sheep in Scotland to shrink

Scientists first began studying Soay sheep, on the island of Hirta in the St Kilda archipelago, in 1985
Classic evolutionary theory would predict that wild sheep gradually get bigger, as the stronger, larger animals survive into adulthood and reproduce.
Reporting in Science journal, the team says this shows the "subtle interplay" between evolution and the environment.
"In the past, only the big, healthy sheep and large lambs that had piled on weight in their first summer could survive the harsh winters on Hirta," said Professor Coulson.
Because of climate change, he explained, grass for food is now available for more months of the year on the island.
"Survival conditions are not so challenging - even the slower growing sheep have a chance of making it, and this means smaller individuals are becoming increasingly prevalent in the population," he said.
The team also found that younger sheep tended to give birth to smaller lambs - a phenomenon they termed "the young mum effect".

From: Johann Wentzel
Sent: Tue 07/07/2009 14:28
42. Subject: What a terrible game of Rugby

Thoughts come and thoughts go as do irritations and piles and those individuals that bring it on. But it is quite difficult to wait long enough for them to just 'go'. The whole story about the rope - sometimes I want to give them the 'enough rope'.

It is raining in Northern Ireland, the heat wave broken and my spirit up, so '*Die Kaap is weer Hollands*'.

There is also a rope bridge in Northern Ireland - well worth a fleeting visit and to cross even if just to say that you have done it: crossing the bridge that is.

Are there really people out there that watch the 'crossing over' programs on TV? What next, a photo of MJ's ghost in Neverland?
Oops   (http://www.dailymail.co.uk/news/worldnews/article-1197780/Ghost-Michael-Jackson-caught-camera-pacing-corridors-Neverland.html)

It is raining in Northern Ireland as already said and that is the thorn in the flesh: the unnecessary duplication: in the written word, in the spoken word, in the endless mountains of paper demanded by the paperless society to get anything and everything done. And what for? To state the obvious, to peat and repeat ad infinitum, to repeat for the sake of repeating. TG my mood has lifted.

It is appraisal time - like clockwork every six months. Lots of paper, meetings, matrixes, proof and emails brought back to life, six months revisited, dissected, re-investigated and then summarised. But I had mine and I am happy. With the six monthly appraisal that is.

Rather watch Jerry Springer or the Boks playing with white armbands.

PS - The Rope bridge in Northern Ireland - Carrick-a-Rede (Carrick-a-rede means 'rock in the road' so that means I must be a "Carrick").

Credit to Wikipedia

From: Johann Wentzel
Sent: Tue 04/08/2009 18:44
43. Subject: Just listen.

They never stop!
They nag, they moan, they complain, they write to the papers, they stand on soapboxes, they swing placards and they don't work but they moan. They just never stop and the women are even worse.

The English across the Irish Sea that is.

They never ever stop: the weather, the government, each other, the rich, the poor, the war in Afghanistan, the weather, the immigrants, the BBC, the NHS (National Health Service), the police, Northern Rock (a bank), bonuses paid to bankers, banks making a profit, banks losing money, schools, children, airlines, the royals, the government and then the weather.

How can the weathermen possibly get it wrong? What about their holidays in the sun in 2010 if the weathermen can't get it right in 2009? Why is the government allowing immigrants into the country? (I mean, please, who will do the work and pay the taxes?)

Do yourself a favour.
Click on http://www.dailymail.co.uk/news then on any of the main news items and scroll down to read what the intelligent and informed Daily Mail readers have to say: click on best voted, worse voted and put your hands round your neck.

How could they ever have ruled the world?

Not the Irish though, they take what comes their way and that is mainly benefits from the (English) state all the way across the Irish sea:

Houses for unmarried teenage mothers, cars for the disabled, jobseekers allowance, tax-credits for anything that you can possibly think of. There are centres run by the government that assist them to claim benefits, special transport to transport the sick and not so sick to and from hospital appointments.

Anyway, I like the weather, the Labour government is weakly bumbling along and changes everything that they can possibly come up with to accommodate the moaners. It is quite embarrassing how they, the government change direction. The poor soldiers in Afghanistan but mind you it will be just over half a million pound in your pocket if you lose all four limbs. Something like £1500 for a broken nose... and remember NHS is free!

Me? I don't qualify for any benefits, not even if I should fall pregnant but I do get free medical services as I am paying National Insurance! I am from outside the EU you know and therefore no benefits for at least eight years.

It is summer and my hay fever is under control, I have a lady that comes in for three hours every two weeks to clean the house, a gardener that mows the lawn also every two weeks, a pretty Irish woman that feeds me 16 hours a day (but only three or four days a week depending on my condensed working arrangement) and a neigbour that feeds me when the wee Irish woman is not around. I also go for a walk on Wednesday evenings with another neigbour that bakes her own bread...

Strange the Irish and food. One has Breakfast, Dinner, Tea and Supper but I may be wrong. It may be Breakfast, Lunch, Tea and Dinner but it is definitely four full meals a day with tea (not to be confused with the 5 o'clock Tea) a few times during the day and before you go to bed - tea with buns while sitting at the dressed table.

So I am moaning. Moaning about my weight, the somewhat uncomfortable feeling when I try to sleep with a full stomach (the doctor (NHS) has prescript pills for heartburn), the tax I pay (20%), the National Insurance that I pay (some percentage above a certain income) and about the swallows dropping droppings on my windowsill times three, on the step in front of my house, the step at the back door... I also moan about the moaners by voting for the best and the worst and sometimes I even add my own penny's worth and then I moan if the moaners don't agree.

Life is good in Northern Ireland,
The days are long, the sun shines, the potatoes are fresh and we have lots and lots of time for the more serious activities and one wee pretty Irish lady can do more in three hours than any cleaner in three weeks in good old Sunny South Africa.

So why was I homesick last week and the week before that? Maybe because it was Marinette's birthday on the 30th or maybe because everybody moaned so much that nobody listened to me or maybe because the Bokke had two wins in a row. It was only the thought of the wee Wild Irish Girl that stopped me from getting onto the plane. That and all the food.

The church on the corner as one enters my wee village –
Bready:

Take care.

I normally set out some time between 7 & 7:30 every morning from the wee village of Bready with its 47 white double storey houses for the 9.9 mile drive to Londonderry / Derry / the Walled City / work.

Bready a quiet waking village surrounded by fields in different depths of green determined by the sun, the clouds and the animals grazing as I get into my wee plump coloured Fiesta Zetec with just over 42000 miles on the clock. Eskimos may have thirty words for 'snow'. The Irish should have sixty for 'green'. My car is booked for its annual M.O.T. on Friday morning the 11th of September at 09:15.

It takes less than two minutes to get to the main Strabane Londonderry road, an old grey church and graveyard on my immediate right as I stop before turning left towards L'Derry. One can hear the rusty church bells from the spare bedroom on a Sunday morning at precisely ten o'clock. TG I am not a sinner or at least not a believer.

This crossing looks like a prop for *Alice in Wonderland* at the moment with the flags flying this time of the year: a few Union Jacks, a Scottish flag or two (white cross against a blue background), the hand of Ulster, the House of Orange and even a Star of David - colourful and pretty.

Most of my drive is next to the Foyle River on my left and more green hills across the slow moving river. Hills spotted with white sheep and a few buildings. More often than not there will be smoke curling from the chimneys.

Magheramason is about two or three miles down the road: Another small village with a petrol station cum shop and the best homemade ice creams and milk shakes, run by friendly Irish people that also sell emergency heating oil in 20 litre containers. Did you know that one can buy *'red diesel'* at half the price of normal diesel? Red diesel is for farm use only.

I normally meet the first tractor of the day as I leave Magheramason. Big green John Deere tractors pulling tanks of liquid fertilizer on balloon wheels or trailers stacked high with farming produce. The load depends on the time of the year. I have even been privileged to be trapped behind a tractor pulling three wagons in tandem overflowing with potatoes. It may have been Queens or maybe even floury Pinks. I can't be 100% sure.

I normally lose the tractors before reaching firstly the M.O.T. testing grounds and then the village of Newbuildings about three miles further down the road towards work. Newbuildings is a Protestant stronghold and the pavement blocks are painted to complement the flags. It also has a Chinese take-away with a menu that caters for over 100 dishes, all served with either potatoes or rice or half-half. Half-half means half chips half rice.

The Foyle River has a beauty of its own - it may have waves either pushing inland or galloping back towards the ocean. It is a salmon spawning tidal river and I would guess roughly four hundred meters wide. There are at least three clean and well maintained picnic spots right next to the river in the last few miles before one reaches the double-decker bridge that takes you across the river to deposit you into the walled city of Londonderry/Derry. I think the royal blue Craigavon Bridge is actually the only double-decker bridge in the whole of the UK and it does confuse my Garmin satnav (GPS). The upper deck shows inlays of the town's coat of arms in its pillars. I normally use the lower deck. The town's coat of arms is a yellow skeleton against a black background.

The drive takes about twenty minutes depending on tractors or whether I am overcome by the urge to stop at one of the picnic spots. The one just re-opened even has a mounted telescope to look at the sheep, I guess or can one see salmon in the water?

Google maps - Starting point BT82 0EQ to BT48 0GY.

PS - It is my birthday on the 24th in this month of August and the reason for this email.
I will be 57.
I will also be in Switzerland from the Saturday to the Tuesday.
A gift from the wee Irish Girl.
My birthday is on that Monday.

Craigavon Bridge into Londonderry/Derry / Walled City:

If sad is not the word then what is!

The current life expectancy for a woman in the UK is 81,7 years.

One in six Brits are too lazy to get up to change a TV channel.

Many are too lazy to have sex, but then I have been privileged to see quite a few British women and that may just distort the stats. But again, they may just be willing to get up and change the TV channel if you ask nicely.

Did you know the bones of women who drink beer regularly have been found to be stronger and less likely to become brittle?

Anyway, to get back to life expectancy:

I have seen that as well and it is really sad: adult nappies, adult burps, adult walkers, adult meals, adult vitamin supplements, adult care-homes where they try and keep you alive as long as possible by raising the central heating to 30 degrees 24 hours a day, seven days a week. By fitting you with adult nappies, adult burps, adult walkers, adult meals, adult vitamin supplements...

And I have seen a population that is controlled by paranoia. Fear for the sake of fear.

There must be a government plot to control the current economically active population by fear.

Fear has sort of taken over from religion to control the masses. Fear - the opium of the British masses.

Fear for busses running late, trains not arriving, being sued for compensation, compensation claims being rejected, for databases of personal information, fear for the youth or "yobs" as they are called here. (Shame, the poor youngsters are bored so smashing car windscreens and slashing tyres are understandable and excusable) - http://www.dailymail.co.uk/news/article-1205490/Hazel-Blears-car-attacked-canvassing-constituency.html.)

But ultimately, fear for the sake of fear.

And finally the fear of getting old.

Did you know women spend one year and four months of their lives in tears?
Now that is sad.

Don't cry, or if you have to, cry in your beer.

From: Johann Wentzel
Sent: Thu 27/08/2009 09:41
46. Subject: It's a strange strange world we live in Master Jack

It is official: life started from a single cell without the intervention of a creator, but then I knew that all along.

All life started from that one single lonely cell and a new cell can only come from another cell by splitting into two that will split into two that will …

Have been watching a three part series on BBC4 called '*The Cell*'. Well worth the three hours watch time in total.

Then, *Big Brother* on Channel 4 will be cancelled after the next series in 2010 so maybe there is a god.

Apparently *Big Brother* turned older people (the over 44's), off from watching Channel 4 causing revenue loss. That and then it was lately watched mainly by women…

But then, if there was a god, maybe she would have been a woman and I would like to suggest that woman…

Fay Weldon: 'Women would find life easier if they picked up men's socks and cleaned the loo'

She has written a wealth of staunchly feminist books. But it appears old age may even have mellowed Fay Weldon. The veteran author, 77, now claims woman have unrealistic expectations of men and would find life easier if they picked up the socks and cleaned the loo themselves.

Speaking in an interview to promote her latest novel, *Chalcot Crescent*, the prolific author said: "*There are women at work and there's mating behaviour and women get them confused.*"

145

"At work, gender should not come into it. Women are right to refuse to make the coffee, but when you get home I'm afraid you have to make the coffee."

"It's such a waste of time trying to tell your husband to pick up the socks or clean the loo. It's much easier just to do it yourself."

Asked if she thinks feminism has destroyed women, the author of *The Lives and Loves of a She Devil and Puffball* claimed that there are fundamental differences between the sexes.

She added that men should not be given such a hard time by career-minded women.

"Life is much better, because you are not dependent on the goodwill of men," she continued, referring to the growth of women in the workplace.

But the trouble is, the battle became too fierce, and the whole culture encouraged women to believe that men are stupid, useless creatures who are the enemy.

"But men nowadays aren't s***. They're actually much nicer. They just don't want to commit to you, and why would they when you are a busy working woman who can look after yourself and probably goes to bed easily with them?"

Weldon, a mother of four boys who has been married three times, also said women should not expect men to be their best friend - and should appreciate their need for sex.

'The thing is, you need to find a man who is cleverer than you, or at least not let him know that you are cleverer than him,' she said.

"Women want their boyfriends to be like their girlfriends, fun to go to the pictures with, but men are not like that. They

want sex and they grunt."

"If you really want a man to be nice to you, never give him a hard time, never talk about emotions and never ask him how he is feeling."

The outspoken author added that women should have children before they embark on a career and not be so picky about finding the perfect man.

"I think we should have more teenage pregnancies, and work afterwards."

"If you have children late you have no energy left for sex, and then men wander off to find someone else."

"The definition of a good man has become ridiculous. I just think that as long as you have a sort of semi-good looking, able-bodied, intelligent man, you should have his baby."

http://www.dailymail.co.uk/femail/article-1209154/Fay-Weldon-Women-life-easier-picked-mens-socks-cleaned-loo.html

And to think that all that wisdom came from the first and only wee cell.

Didn't the Four Jacks and a Jill venture into gospel music at some stage and lost all their money? That was after they moved down to Knysna to start some farming project for hippies or something. They must be well over 44 by now and hopefully the wiser.

Live and learn.

From: Johann Wentzel
Sent: Thu 03/09/2009 11:52
47. Subject: Isn't it strange that the strange don't see themselves as strange!

I mean, really.

We, some of us from the Hippie generation, may understand earrings and maybe even the odd tattoo or belly ring but really, what have the "strange" ever contributed?
Reality TV, the Greens, Plane Stupid (a UK group that targets airports) and what else? No wars, lots of vegetarians, women body builders looking like men, men smelling like women, children for same sex partners, kissing on the cheek, funny length pants, old men with ponytails...

Anyway, the Irish may be a wee bit peculiar but not strange. They would say that they leave that to the Brits to be strange but then they, the Irish tend to say nothing and only fight with their own. The local saying is that if you insult one Irishman you insult them all - everybody seems to be related to everybody else - a bit like the Afrikaners. But then, it is a small wee island cut off from the rest of the world - a bit like South Africa.

So the Irish summer came and went and it was good while it lasted. We even went down to Galway in the south and stayed at a B&B at Salthill - well worth a visit. A bit like the Durban of my youth. Google "*Galway*" and eat your heart out.

It is about a five or six hour drive from Linda's place via Enniskillen, Sligo and a few other wee Irish villages with

149

narrow one way streets and colourful flowerbeds: very scenic with no nonsense cafes dotted along the main route. A place where you can get a warm mug of tea and a scone slapped on a plastic table cloth in front of you - straight from the farm kitchen. Take it or leave it. My kind of people.

We also stopped at a more formal coffee shop in Sligo - run by a Frenchman married to an Irish girl. Quite a talkative guy with photos of him surfing off the Irish coast pasted on the walls of his coffee bar. Also makes interesting sandwiches and buns - anything and everything sweet is called a "bun" here. My wee bun is called Linda and her Afrikaans is really improving. This is more and more like home from home without some of the home comforts like traffic jams, 60 hour weeks, power cuts, etc. By the way, I am so disappointed with *Die Beeld* newspaper - they upgraded their online website and what a disaster, does not make for easy reading now!

Galway was interesting - lots of strange people from all over the world. You know the type - Americans hanged with cameras, wide-rimmed hats and flowery shirts. Also people speaking strange languages in funny high pitched voices. A wee bit expensive mind you, but it was Linda's treat to me for my birthday as we had to cancel the Switzerland trip at the very last moment: blame it on the Swiss, the EU or the Souf African government but they, the Swiss have changed the rules. We Souf Africans now require Schengen Visas to enter Switzerland! That is as from December 2008.

I went through a bit of an identity crisis after that - felt like a second class citizen that has lost my dompass! Wanted to get onto the first plane and go straight back to South Africa

150

but that would have been plane stupid. I have now been here for over three years.

We came back from Galway via a placed called Cong where the movie, "*The Silent Man*" was filmed in 1951.
John Wayne starred in it - notice the initials JW. Not all that we have in common - I am also the Silent Type.

So without further ado.

'We are very good at seeking out meaning and patterns in randomness - it's one of the reasons humans are such a successful species. But the price is that we see significance in things that aren't there at all."

Anyway, I killed two swallows: a mother and the baby. But, I am not too sure about the mother. But then, what are (were) they still doing in Northern Ireland? It is already autumn here and surely that must mean spring has sprung in South and Southern Africa.

Don't come with that cr*p about them being confused by Climate Change and bull-dust like that - I don't believe any of that. I am an educated, barely into middle age man that do think for himself. As one of my new friends said (he is actually retired, owns a house in Knysna and is on the one or other government advisory board to do with climate change) it is all due to the increase in the number of livestock - cows. Apparently their f*rting are killing the ozone layer and I have not smelled a thing.

Anyway, I got home last night and had to once again climb the **S**wallow **D**roppings **M**ountain to slide into my wee entrance hall. So I took out my long pole and jabbed the swallow nest to see what reaction I will get. Out popped an irritated wee swallow chicken, all upset and I immediately put my pole away as if caught in some activity that should not be done in public. A quarter of the nest was however destroyed and now adding to the height of the SDM. I felt terrible and went back inside to clean my shoes - enough qwana to feed all my houseplants. I also prayed that the wind will die down, that it will not rain (this is Ireland) and that the daddy swallow will return and rebuilt the nest.

It did not rain. I don't know about the wind, I was sleeping, but I could barely open the front door this morning. The daddy did not rebuild the nest - he must have left for sunnier shores. There was however two dead swallows on top of the ever growing SDM! One a wee fat fluffy swallow chick not ready to fly yet.

I had a quick funeral and was nearly 15 minutes later at work than normal! I should have broken the nest when they first started it - would have saved the parents the trouble of raising a chick for six months just for it to meet an early black municipal wheelie bin grave.

Isn't it interesting: the story about Winston the homing pigeon that beat the SA internet in delivering 4GB of data from Howick to Hillcrest in just over two hours?
They could have done better - they could have used a man dressed as a woman carrying a cleft stick to do it in less than two hours.

So 09/09/09 came and went (nearly) and this wee planet is still going around the sun, that is going around who knows what, that is revolving around who knows what and I should be fine as long it is not all controlled by some swallow somewhere sitting on an even bigger SDM.

PS:
Isn't it interesting that 999 is also the UK's emergency

154

number! Pity swallows can't phone or send pigeons.

PSS:
Did you know the world population will officially reach 6.8 billion near November 2009 and that Revelation 6.8 is about the fourth horseman, Death? So, there is still hope for planet earth if swine flu or aids would just mutate.

Winter has arrived - seven o'clock this morning, Wednesday the 14th of October.

It is really '*nice*'! The drive to work started when it was still dark - sort of.
Little spits of rain on the windscreen and red lights tailing along the beautiful calm river Foyle: all under a winter warm grey low hanging blanket.

I also had to go home at lunch time to meet with the builder - he is putting in some soundproofing (place is still under guarantee).
Dear old neigbour must think we Souf Africans have strange roaring stomachs. All that I can think and don't forget - it is a semi-dethatched wee double storey.

Anyway, I asked her whether I may stay over at her place tonight seeing that I had to move all the furniture out of my bedrooms, but "*what will the people say*" so I will be sleeping amongst builder rubble tonight - all warm and cozy with the central heating on. I mean, I am harmless. I am a South African and don't know about being politically correct - what we say is what we mean and what we do.

Anyway, it was still dark - sort of when I came back at lunch time today, this Wednesday the 14th of October just after 1 o'clock.

Winter has its own beauty in Northern Ireland. The air is

157

brisk and clear even when it is grey.

Strange place this: all the houses are painted in dull colours. Must be part of being politically correct - nobody wants to be seen as being different.

Be that as it may - people have started lighting their fires and one can now order hot soup and fresh bread for lunch.

The bedroom windows have streaks of condensation pooling on the windowsill when you open the curtains in the morning, so the central heating not only heats the house but it also dries it out if you leave the windows just a wee bit open. All (just about) houses have double glazing. I do however prefer to use the central heating sparingly to firstly save a few pence and secondly I don't like it too hot.

I must admit, the whole place does have a romantic or an early Christmas feel to it: each house a wee paradise of soft glowing light and welcoming heat hovering somewhere between the dark green fields and grey dirty cottonwood heavens. A real aura of peace and tranquillity. All children's bicycles and toys have disappeared from the pavements and babies are wrapped in blankets and propped up in buggies with transparent plastic covers. Too pretty to look into a pram and see a wide-eyed pink little face peeking back at you with not a squeak out of it. The milk in Ireland is rich and the containers beautiful - winter or summer!

Work has slowed to a trickle down but I am still gainfully employed.

The wee Irish woman is still madly in love with me and adds

to the warmth in my heart.

My car passed its MOT, so is fine for another year. I also had to pay the car insurance for the next year - just a few pence under £300-00.

I am also paying an instalment of just under £120.00 per month and who knows, Father Christmas may just bring me a new wee car - a Mazda2 or Getz will do.

Petrol varies but comes to about £1.10 per litre.

Anyway, it is time to go home and it is still dark… It is 6 o'clock and my neigbour has invited me for a bite to eat - to discuss the noise next door no doubt.

Take care and sleep warm - even in summer.

From: Johann Wentzel
Sent: Wed 09/12/2009 18:36
50. Subject: Early Christmas wishes

Early Christmas wishes - it is the company's Christmas evening tomorrow, Thursday the 10th of December 2009 and they will only pay for the first five drinks!
I complain best when I have nothing to complain about.
I am also such a positive person.
Always ready, and more than willing, to give every doomsday prophet my full support.
Just once, is all that I am asking for. Just once do I wish them to be proven right.

I was all for the 1994 elections, the Y2K bug, the Da Vinci Code, the climate fiasco...
I have embraced the *Swart Gevaar*, the *Red Gevaar*, the Nationalist Party.
I was more than ready for a world without oil, for MIR falling on my head, for aliens landing, for women having the vote.
You name it and I was there. I even bought a book called "*Have a happy doomsday*" (strange that they insisted on upfront payment).

Life is so good to me. Has always been and will also be. We Irish may even have a white Christmas (We did win the Rugby).
It is currently dark between three in the afternoon and eight in the morning.
Dark and wet, but my oil tank is full and my electric blanket plugged in.
I still work a four day week, still get fed by the friendly neigbour at least twice a week.

Still go down to Waringstown for a three day long weekend and I have bought a new wee car to be delivered just before Christmas.
It is a white 4-door Ford Fiesta 1.6 Econetic, the UK's greenest family car. Google it.
The most fuel efficient car on the road doing something like 80 miles to a gallon and currently the only car on the UK roads where one does not have to pay road tax as its CO_2 emission is less than 100g/km.

The wee Irish girl is still mad about me and about Africa and I about her. You should see the framed photos of our two trips (safaris as they call it here) into darkest Africa on the walls of her house. Also photos of our skiing trip to Italy and photos of birthdays and previous Christmases.

Her capacity for all things good and clean and fresh is just unbelievable. Her heart a treasure. I am a lucky man.

So let us raise our eyes to the heavens and hope and pray for the 21st of December 2012. But until then, have a blessed Christmas.

PS - According to their calendar, the Maya believed that their world would end on Dec 21, 2012.

So I have relocated / transferred to Belfast and am settling in nicely - there is a staff canteen at the new Belfast office that serves a bowl of Oats porridge and a cup of filter coffee for £1.70. It is £1.40 when you have a small cup of instant coffee.

Lunch comes with lots of potato and can cost you anything up to £5.00 I guess (cheap at the price). A full plate of chips with beans and cheese is £2.20.

Food is important - it has been freezing cold since I can't recall when - but then, I have only been in Northern Ireland since July 2006.

Belfast is worth a visit and I am not talking about the Belfast on the way to the Kruger. This is Belfast, the undisputed capital of Northern Ireland.

Did you know that the guy that wrote about Lilliput (Gulliver's Travels) got his inspiration from the wee hill in the shape of a man on his back that I can see from my new office?

The new office is much bigger that the office in Londonderry / Derry with about a thousand or so people. How many actually work, I can't tell.

The people are also not as friendly as the lot up in L'Derry - more a big city temperament but I make up for that with my sunny Souf African personality.

I am still finding my way around - go out at lunch times for a wee slip down the frozen pavements, blowing my own clouds with jaw that stops functioning after 30 seconds flat.

It is quite interesting looking at the other people slip sliding away. It is so cold that my glasses fog up when I get back into the office.

Everything is however crisp and crystal clear when it is not snowing and not raining. That however does not mean that the sun is shining - it is still winter.

Lots of old buildings and pubs all over Belfast with a good university - Queens University. Even a Nando's and a Spur - what more can a man possibly ask for.

And I do get lost - walking and driving. TG for my Satnav else I will not be able to find my way home to Waringstown and will freeze to death once the wee new white car runs out of diesel. I am still trying to determine the best mode of transport into Belfast - car, train or bus. Have used the train twice and the car three times. Still to use the bus but think it will be the train even though I have to drive about 10 kilometers from Waringstown to Moira to catch the train - I left home this morning at 06:45 and was seated at my desk at 07:50, so not too bad. The train journey is a real pleasure with comfortable seats and a wee table between you and the pleasant young lady with the cold cleavage opposite. I am more and more convinced it must have something to do with the rich creamy milk in Northern Ireland. Either that or the big fresh Irish potatoes!

Had to wait until nearly nine before I could have my bowl of Oats and my cup of filter coffee.

On the work front - I don't know whether I am coming or going. We are in the midst of a restructure. The team is being split into Production Support (PS) and Run the Business (RTB) and I am now suppose to do Production Support only - one of those things where the paper trail becomes more important that the actual work. It is driven from the States and is due to a cost saving exercise that will cost millions to implement before it will die a slow and painful death with lots of high-fives and promotions all around. But then, I have been there before.

My house in Bready has been unofficially declared a disaster area and I will not be able to move back for at least six and maybe eight weeks. All due to the burst water-pipe in the attic - strange country this. Strange how things always come together. Me moving to Waringstown and now working from Belfast and the house in Bready falling to the elements.

I asked for a transfer just before Christmas and it came through within a few days. This was all done and dusted before the pipe sprang a leak. So I am quit contented with the way that thinks have worked out - not happy with the flooding but happy being in Waringstown.

Linda's dad is seriously ill in hospital and I don't think he will ever go home again except if "*home*" is heaven. The family was asked on numerous occasions whether the doctors should attempt to restart his heart if it should stop or whether they should start feeding him directly into his stomach - the answer was "no" to both questions.

I have to resubmit my papers to the UK Home Office in the next week or so to get my visa reconfirmed / re-issued / rejected due to all the changes. It may take some time as there is an election on the horizon and both main political parties have promised a drastic cut in immigration - wonder who will do the work in this wee Island?

Regards to all and keep warm.

By the way - there is no heaven and TG also no hell.

From: Johann Wentzel
Sent: Mon 18/01/2010 17:39
52. Subject: A burst water pipe, a flooded house, lots of food and a funeral

Hi *Mense.*

The land of milk and honey this is.

And bread, snacks, buns, a lake of coffee and an ocean of tea!

It was like Park Station or maybe a Venter trailer heading north over the Easter Weekend - packed to overflow: my poor stomach that is.

Linda's Dad passed away last Wednesday evening just after 11 o'clock. We were at his bedside from about 12 that morning after the hospital phoned to say that he was knocking on the door. I was at home with Linda's Mom when he finally passed away - his three children, Linda, Craig and Julie were at his side.

The old man turned 85 in November last year and had a good life. I was one of the bearers at the funeral. He could not have weight more than 6 stone but then he stood only 5' 2.5" high.

It was interesting going through his personal papers afterwards. He had quite a life, the old man - there must have been forty photos if not more of him with some girl at his side. A different girl every time. He was the second of six children. His Mom died at childbirth when he was thirteen, he started work at sixteen and he went to Australia when he was in his late twenties to work as a porter on the Australian railways to send money home to support his younger two

167

sisters. There was no work in Ireland after the war.

He even kept the original ticket for the journey - that came to 10 pounds and the trip itself took five weeks sailing via the Suez Canal. He did not pay for the trip. It was sponsored by the Australian government and only had to be repaid if you didn't complete, I think three years of work down under.

Back to last week and Northern Ireland - He was in hospital for a week before he died - it was for the better in the end even though he had the "best" possible medical care as he was really suffering and not able to swallow, but that is another email altogether. Enough to say that I don't agree with too much medical intervention when you are 85 and the end is there for all to see.

As far as the Irish - It could have been South-West Africa (Namibia for the new generation) in the good old days: people, people and more people arriving with fresh sandwiches and buns (buns are things like cup-cakes, Scottish shortbread, cream thingies, coconut thingies, jam thingies, custard thingies, small cakes, not so small cakes, big cakes, etc.). Some people brought whole sliced loafs of bread & ready spreads, instant coffee and sealed boxes of tea bags. The neigbours offered their driveways for parking and the door stood open from morning to evening with the kettle on the boil 24 hours out of 24.

It was quite touching and very much appreciated by the family - I count myself as one of the family and was treated as such - quite touching. I was fond of the old man and he of me - kept on asking Linda how her husband is (that's me!). Used to watch old John Wayne movies together while he

168

would have a pint and I would have something softer and Linda ironing - the Irish women can only work! My poor stomach still can't handle too much of the Irish full milk or Guinness!

Who knows - I may just be wrong. The Irish may actually be God's chosen people and not the Afrikaners.

Anyway, the whole thing once again opened my eyes to how important family and friends are when the potatoes are down. Have been dreaming about Werner, Elbereth, M & M, Ty and lots of new babies ever since so it must be time for another trip to Surrey and to Cape Town. There is however the small "issue" of the UK home office at the moment. But then, all things come to them that wait, I guess!

The funeral was from Linda's house on Saturday afternoon - the minister, a pleasant young lady and soft on the eye, came to the house for the actual service. She wore a powder blue top with one of those wrong-way-round collars that the clergymen wear. I actually felt a wee bit sorry for her (touched by her seemingly genuine conviction of another life hereafter, but this is neither the place nor the time).

The old man was buried from the house - the undertakers delivered the remains early on Thursday afternoon after we had prepared the formal dining room for that - soft music (Susan Boyle), dimmed lights and the central heating turned down.

After the service at home, attended by about a hundred people, the body was carried shoulder high from the estate to the main street where it was transferred to the hearse - a brand new black Jaguar. Must have been at least a V8 - double exhausts - we were the first car behind it. All town traffic came to a standstill as we drove to the cemetery where we had to carry the coffin to the grave - shoulder high once again.

The pleasant young lady priest then delivered a final short service at the actual grave side. A double grave that was bought on Thursday morning. It allows for six - two groups of three… It can only be bought when needed and not in advance. It is however now available for the next five services.

TG it was not raining or snowing Saturday afternoon. There was even a bit of sunshine, but still bone chilling cold. The cemetery itself is a headstones only cemetery, so it looked more like a quite park than a cemetery in the grey but clear rain washed Saturday afternoon light with the odd bit of slippery ice still to be seen on the ground.

Everybody then dispersed to the local hotel for soup, more sandwiches and even more tea.

My wee semi-detached two storey house up in Bready is still not liveable - had a call earlier today from the assessor to inform me that the downstairs floor tiles will definitely have to be lifted. The ceilings were taken down and the carpets lifted last week, the furniture will be stored and the place should be dried out in 28 days or so - the de-humidifiers were delivered on Friday last week and are going full blast.

I am going for a wee medical procedure on Wednesday morning so that means that I will be working from the

Allstate Northland office (Londonderry / Derry) for part of Wednesday at least - having a wee black thingy removed from my skin just under my left ear but it is at the day clinic so I should be as right as sunshine in an hour or so - also have to go for a haircut, pick up my post, visit the chemist, my friendly neigbour, have a look at the flooded house in Bready and attempt to see the dentist for a check-up already booked. All things that will eventually follow me to Waringstown and / or Belfast.

I must be getting old but then maybe not.

Take care,

Ty was one year old this week, it is still slippery cold in Northern Ireland (so much so that I couldn't wind down my driverside window yesterday when I went home as it was frozen shut), Elbereth is in Mexico for her work and Barry at their place in Limpsfield, Oxted, Surrey just outside London and Michael & Marinette braai every day cause they stay in Cape Town, that quite clean wee village some distance from Johannesburg. Isn't life great! I saw even Zuma had a wee snooze in parliament.

The builder is still fixing my wee semi-detached two storey 3-bedroom white house, but I have instructed the letting agent to roundup a tenant hopefully from the 1st of March 2010. Will take some pressure off my financial situation.

I have a multiple entry Schengen visa (valid 24 March to 20 August) and will travel. *Why is the world so horrible towards us peace loving Souf Africans*?
Anyway, I am off to Switzerland at the end of March, then Spain first week in May and South Africa towards the end of the year.
My car is going really well - deep throat sound like a tractor!
There is lots of oil in the tank for the central heating.
The hot water geyser comes on as set and there are fresh potatoes in the kitchen.
The Six Nations have started.
The wee wild Irish Girl is going from strength to strength.
I don't have a gardener, nor a servant to feed, to pay and to worry about. Life is really great.

"**Galway Bay**" by Arthur Colahan

If you ever go across the sea to Ireland,
Then maybe at the closin' of your day
You will sit and watch the moon rise over Claddagh
And see the sun go down on Galway Bay.

[And if there's to be a life in the hereafter --
And somehow I'm sure there's going to be --
I will ask my God to let me make my heaven
In that dear land across the Irish sea.

Just to hear again the ripple of the trout stream
And the women in the meadows making hay,
To sit beside the turf fire in the cabin
And watch the barefoot gossoons at their play.

For the breezes blowin' across the sea from Ireland
Are perfumed by the heather as they blow.
And the women in the upland diggin' praties
Speak a language that the strangers do not know.

*For the **strangers** came and tried to teach us their way.*
They scorned us just for bein' what we are.
But they might as well go chasin' after moon beams
Or light a penny candle from a star.

And if there's to be a life in the hereafter --
And somehow I'm sure there's going to be --
I will ask my God to let me make my heaven,
In that dear land across the Irish sea.]

The *strangers* are the English!

174

Note:
I am cleaning out my contact list and you will be deleted from it if I don't get a reply instructing me otherwise.
Family are not that lucky - they are stuck with me.

Take care and have a warm weekend!

PS:
We bought a two plot (double) six body grave in the cemetery at Lurgan - really cool!

"Koud is die windjie
En skraal
En dof in die maanlig
En kaal."

Sien, ek kan nog my trotse laerskool gedigte onthou of ten minste 'n gedeelte!

It could have been Ireland.
It is still cold, but our (summer) day will come.
That day of summer when we will all go '*kaal*' to soak up the sun.
When the earth will burst open.
Actually, come to think of it, the smell of "burst" manure did fill my nose last week.
A smell like no other.

I went to boarding school in Windhoek, Namibia in 1966 through 1967 and Windhoek recycles all water - even to this day and that was why Ben Geldenhuys' dad used to have two big stainless steel milk drums and a mug made form an old coffee tin, on the back of the bakkie. For those trips to Windhoek. But back to Windhoek and the recycled water - all water. And by all, I really mean all.

The solids were (are) deposited about 10 kilometers out of town at a place called Bokkiesdraai and it had (has) a real unique smell - and then the wind would begin to blow (a bit like the Vitalis hair oil advert before the time of TV) and all

177

car windows would be closed: even on a 40 plus degree mid summers dry dusty African day. And the adults would become irritated and the children would say: "*Eerste geruik gaatjie gebruik, tweede geruik eiertjie gelê*" and the irritated adults would turn around and smack all and sundry. *Aai*, the good old days; before car air conditioners and children with human rights.

But this '*planting*' smell. This Irish season smell is even more unique and it can linger, hang in the air, cling to your palate.

It must spring from the deepest deep soul of the potato, fermented in dark Guinness over many cold moons. It can take paint off a car, I think. It makes dogs bury their noses in the mud. And I tighten all backside muscles when I smell it and I laugh out loud through clenched jaws. It is that sort of smell. A smell that makes you run back into the house to share the experience with your nearest and dearest!

So now I am sharing with you, because this smell makes one realises that one is alive. And what is life but for sharing!

I have a boring existence and it suites me down to the ground.

I eat, I sleep and I am. I enjoy my walk to and from work; to/from where I park my wee white car with a diesel beat like a green John Deere tractor, finely tuned. To work just after seven in the mornings and from work just after six at night - four days a week. Remember, I work condensed hours so that means a four day week with the Friday off for four

178

weeks in a row and then the Monday off four times and then back to Fridays. It was just extended for another year to the end of Feb 2011. May there be another grandchild before then!

A ten to fifteen minute walk, depending on my mood - the quick route next to the river, then cross over via the pedestrian bridge and down past the big old parking building being renovated Or the longer but more scenic route where I first head away from the Allstate building once I have crossed the river to walk between the Hilton hotel and the river just to swing back around the hotel building back, back to Allstate.

Or the third way: crossing the river with the cars over the main bridge to the feet of the lady with the hoop and then sharp left next to the river all the way top the office - the Belfast fish behind me.

I will switch on the lights on the ground floor south when I get to the offices - I am normally in first. Two rows of four switches. Only the top row as I discovered after a few attempts. There is some sort of build in delay and you use the same switch action to both turn the lights on and off.

Then turn on my wee computer or "*boot it*" as I like to say. Scan my emails, phone Linda to wake her, fill my water bottle and go out for a wee cup of coffee.

A cup of coffee that would normally include a wee something to eat as well. (I do miss Wimpy though!). And a quick page through the paper - I also miss "Die Beeld".

But the lady at the café is friendly and once said: "*I love your accent, I can listen to it the whole day*", so now I just point and say very little - true to my nature.

Point to the porridge (oats) with honey (£1.95) or the mini fry (£3.95) or the full fry (£4.95) or a wee brown bread toastie of cheese and red onion (£3.75).

Coffee, I am not a great coffee drinker but this coffee is the best in the world, if not Northern Ireland. (£1.35 if you sit down, else the early morning special take out price of 99 pence.)

Then back to work for more emails (I average hundred plus a day and also monitor the incident mailbox), to update my time sheet plus three - this is s paperless society so just to make sure, make sure we have three time recording systems: one for billing purposes, one for the Americans and one to record activity status - and to sign onto the mainframe and do some work.

I am now going to do some work.

The next boring chapter to follow in a day or two or who knows. In a week or two.

Take care and don't forget the sun-block. Spring is on us!

The Belfast fish:

From: Johann Wentzel
Sent: Mon 01/03/2010 11:57
55. Subject: 1 March 2010

What else could I do? I just kept on walking - one foot on the pavement, one on the road. Not after the friendly older lady put a £1.00 coin in my hand as I reached out to press the pedestrian button (really to catch my breath before crossing the main road in Belfast centre).

I have mentioned the walking Irish (women) before. It still intrigues me after three and a half year, as I was once again overtaken this morning. This time by a blind woman as I was on my way to work.
Well, I guess her all-seeing dog overtook me and I ended up in a total state of panic. This dog, a yellow tail wagging, nose close to the pavement, Labrador, was going at neck breaking speed - keeping up with the rest of the people and overtaking me, weaving in and out between the three feet high black painted barriers with their three red reflective warning stripes at the top and I was convinced this girl was going to end up impaled in one of these things - what to do? Walk faster and overtake them as not to see blood spattered all over the pavement (impossible - I was going flat out - one foot high, one foot low) or slow down even further and make it someone else's cleanup problem?

But the dog and flying blind woman managed and left me standing. And I had the shorter direct route to follow.

It is the 1st of March today, Saint David's day and the first day of our Spring or is it?.Well, that depends on who you talk to: Some say today is the official start of Spring. Others say it only starts in about two weeks or so. We Irish never agree on anything. Anyway, it is definitely St David's day - the patron saint of Wales and the sun is shining. Will have to find my wee cap and keep it in the car if not on my head.

I still get the weather wrong after three and a half years - still think it must be warm when the sun shines. Still think I will not get caught in the rain when I go out for a quick 8 minutes to get a sandwich. Still think I can get into the car and drive off without first defrosting the windscreen. Still think I can open the garbage bin early in the morning on my way to work without getting my hand stuck frozen to the lid. Still think I will understand (or be understood) when I answer the phone. So, the bottom line - every day is still an adventure in this most beautiful wee island in the whole wide world.

My wee semi-detached house is still being fixed - should get the go-ahead for the carpets today or tomorrow and the place may just be habitable again in a week or two.
What an expensive wet disaster this has turned out to be!

And then we are off to Switzerland at the end of March for a few days - the sun may be shining there as well. Then to Spain the first week in May - the sun will be shining and I will take my cap with me (and my umbrella).

So why am I relating all this to you? Pure and simple. To make you all jealous! And because I can't be in South Africa in April for the wedding - just no money Honey.

Take care and remember we all agree: Today is the first day of Autumn in Sunny South Africa.

Hallo julle daar ver oor die water!

It is such a nice day today here in Belfast, the capital city of Northern Ireland. Was a flashing 3 degrees (*possibility of ice on the road*) this morning and a forecasted high of 11. Spring has indeed sprung, but I don't think it quite got to 11 degrees. Maybe tomorrow, my day off due to my condensed working agreement.

3-degrees - Just right for my brisk walk from the car park to the office at seven in the morning: about 8 minutes but then I don't have time to look at the Lagan River making its much slower way in the opposite direction pass Samson and Goliath, the two great yellow-painted cranes that everybody should know about. Part of Belfast's skyline and history, or the river Lagan that I have to cross twice a day to get to work and my car. (It actually froze over in January this year.)

I park in a 'friend's' spot at his apartment block - $35.00 a month. How can 'friends' charge you for using their vacant parking spot? Open parking, so there are times when I have to scrape the ice off the windscreen of my wee white four-door car with the deep tractorlike roar. Love it to bits and it still smells new! Is there anything in this world that smells as nice?

Well, maybe Linda's hair when she comes out of the shower or her special chilly chicken and cream dish or when she gets back into bed on a Saturday morning. She is such a treasure - and she sometimes sounds as if she has a wee diesel engine somewhere deep in her chest. Not that she herself ever hears that!

We, Linda and I have started cycling - covered ten miles on our first official trip out next to the Newry canal and just under three miles on the second trip around one of the numerous lakes here in Northern Ireland. Really a land of milk and honey and water.

It is flat and easy going next to water, even when one goes against the flow of the water and nearly three miles sounds better than two-and-a-half. But then it started raining. Just as we were finishing our intimate little picnic of sweet hot tea, sandwiches, yoghurt.

Who knows - we may just have another picnic next to the water tomorrow or Saturday - it is Spring with lots of yellow daffodils. Linda is working on Sunday. She also took my car today to have a tow bar fitted; will make transporting our two bicycles that much easier.

I have a choice of routes to and from work, depending on the weather, the time, my mood and my workload.

I can either go the wolf's way across the pedestrian bridge next to the railways that takes about 8 minutes; the way across the river using either of the two main bridges and then decide whether to walk next to the river just about all the way or to cut across and use the old metal gate that opens at seven in the morning and closes at seven at night.

I normally tend to take one of the longer routes at night - gives me time clear my head, to smile at the Irish, to eye the girls and the mad people rowing (punting) on the river Lagan. I have no decision to make for the last few hundred yards (we are English) if it is after seven o'clock. It is not only the church bells and illuminated old clocks that keep accurate time here.

There are quite a few eating / take out (we are part of the EU) places and an in-house canteen where I get my breakfast and lunch.

There is a small O'Brien's about 45 meters (I am still a South African) from my desk where a very friendly Polish girl knows my order without asking - the breakfast toastie on brown and a cup of latte. All for £2.95. She has been here in Northern Ireland for about the same length of time as me and is about half my age minus 3.

And I have discovered that Boots, the pharmacy (or is that chemist?) has a meal-deal: that is a snack (few strips of fruit that equals one of your five-a-day), a cold drink / fruit juice and a sandwich for £2.99.

"Boots" is about a mile from the office and takes me via the Belfast city hall, so I am getting lots of exercise and fresh air.

Wonder why I am still weighing nearly 107 kilograms?

Plus, I have to go for a liver biopsy in roughly four months time - sort of the average time that one waits for National Health Service specialist treatment if it is not urgent.
I do have company funded private health as well, but have never used it. Guess a biopsy is better than an autopsy any day.

Take care and sometimes take the time to walk the fairy way.

From: Johann Wentzel
Sent: Wed 26/05/2010 14:16
57. Subject: But Newcastle in Northern Ireland is much much closer

Hi My Friend and others!

"And remember - it's the pen that's bad
Don't lay the blame on me."
All will become ocean clear to him (or her) that waits.

We had our two-and-a-half days of summer so we went to Newcastle on Sunday to walk on the beach and to eat lots and lots of ice creams - *'pokes'* as the Irish call them. Lots and lots, remember Linda's Mother suffers badly from Dementia and kept on demanding "a wee *'poke*"!

Also, it is Newcastle in Northern Ireland and not Newcastle in the United Kingdom or even Sunny South Africa. But it could have been S.S.A., except that it was really clean. It was a nice warm pleasant day (with lots and lots of *pokes*).

Temperature touching 30 degrees when we left home with a wee soft breeze that barely ruffled my hair from the ocean that dipped it to the lower twenties when we got to Newcastle. The tide was out; the waves but babies and a dove white sail yacht half way to the pale blue horizon. The mirror ocean different shades of blue / green and the *'sweetest girl I know'* at my side.

So we repeated it yesterday – Tuesday:
I left work early, went to Waringstown to pick up the wee sweetest girl and made our way back to Newcastle Northern

Ireland - about a 45 minute drive from Waringstown. It is all about quality and if one can combine quantity, the cup overflows.

So the new UK coalition government has announced a cap on immigration:
Some background figures first - facts for the programmers amongst us:
Net immigration was 150 000 last year.
There were 100 000 non-EU immigrants - that included their dependants.
It was not mentioned how many non-EU immigrants actually remained in the country, but anyway, this is the way of politics.
The new government will cap net immigration to 100 000 this year, BUT they (the government) can't limit immigration from the EU.
We are all bright. "*We*" being my friend and others. We can all do the sums.

My passport is currently with the UK Home Office: posted it Tuesday the 11th of May so should have it back with a new VISA in about six weeks/months or so - these things take time, you know. The government also promised to cut the civil service.

I have also finally found a tenant for my house in Bready - a couple and toddler. They should move in this coming weekend. The rent covers about half my monthly mortgage repayment - think the story of half an egg (or is that a bad translation from Afrikaans?). Anyway, the new coalition government may just end up with a pretty wee rebuilt, repainted, re-carpeted semi-detached white double storey house in Bready with a negative equity of £30 000 plus if the UK Home Office makes a mistake re my claim to stay in this most beautiful island in the world. With that and the tears of the sweetest girl I know. A wee ocean indeed it will be.

I quite like the noises that the new government is making. I am serious! But then, I am also looking forward to the end of the world on the 21st of December 2012 and to the day when Mugabe will admit that he was wrong. Or was he? Wasn't it the British government that went back on their word?

Life in Ireland is still good to me.
Work has picked up quite a lot and all jokes aside - I am not concerned about my papers at the Home Office. I will be 58 this year - still a few months to go. But I have learned that things always turn out for the better.

I am more concerned that Tyro, the dozing dog will destroy my passport when it is dropped through the letterbox one of these fine days. That will not be the first time that I lost my passport - the last time was when it was posted back from the UK mainland and it got lost in the post - only an empty envelope completed the journey across the Irish Sea. That was the best thing that could have happened. I had to have it replaced of course, but it was also extended at the same time and I was then issued with one of the new UK visas instead of just a Rorschach ink blot that is now interpreted at length when you enter the country.

We, Linda and I, are planning a trip down south for the first week of July – "south" is the Republic of Ireland. Our world is our wee world and somewhat smaller than the real world.

Then a trip to Sunny South Africa at the end of August or sometime in September - this will include a week in Namibia to "show Linda where I grew up". This however depends on what Elbereth plans to do - if she is getting married as she said she may, then the trip will have to wait. We, Linda and I are flying to Gatwick London the second week of June to visit with Barry and Elbereth and all will then become clear.

Did you know there is really a place called Timbuktu? Did you know that Tipperary is an actual place and that it is down south?

It's a Long Way to Tipperary

Up to mighty London came
An Irish lad one day,
All the streets were paved with gold,
So everyone was gay!
Singing songs of Piccadilly,
Strand, and Leicester Square,
'Til Paddy got excited and
He shouted to them there:

It's a long way to Tipperary,
It's a long way to go.
It's a long way to Tipperary
To the sweetest girl I know!
Goodbye Piccadilly,
Farewell Leicester Square!
It's a long long way to Tipperary,
But my heart's right there.

Paddy wrote a letter
To his Irish Molly O',

Saying, "Should you not receive it,
Write and let me know!
If I make mistakes in "spelling",
Molly dear", said he,
"Remember it's the pen, that's bad,
Don't lay the blame on me".

It's a long way to Tipperary,
It's a long way to go.
It's a long way to Tipperary
To the sweetest girl I know!
Goodbye Piccadilly,
Farewell Leicester Square,
It's a long long way to Tipperary,
But my heart's right there.

Molly wrote a neat reply
To Irish Paddy O',
Saying, "Mike Maloney wants
To marry me, and so
Leave the Strand and Piccadilly,
Or you'll be to blame,
For love has fairly drove me silly,
Hoping you're the same!"

It's a long way to Tipperary,
It's a long way to go.
It's a long way to Tipperary
To the sweetest girl I know!
Goodbye Piccadilly,
Farewell Leicester Square,

It's a long long way to Tipperary,
But my heart's right there.

From:	Johann Wentzel
Sent:	Tue 20/07/2010 12:13
58. Subject:	Floods and other animals

Ja Mense, ek leef nog!

It is just that I am now living on Irish time - a bit like African time, just much slower. It is also much greener and wetter than South Africa and quite warm at the moment - 20 plus degrees with thunder and lots and lots of rain. Thunder gets the people talking, so I guess they will be shouting from under their beds if we (they) ever experience a good old Joburg afternoon thunder storm. Even a stranger in the shop asked me whether I was woken by the thunder at 4 o'clock this morning. I though it was a naughty neigbour that allowed his wheelie bin to fall over!

The locals always talk about the weather. Everybody is an expert and everybody watches the weather reports and refers to the weather presenters by their first names.

But then, I can recall a time when mirrors were covered, one was not allowed to get into the bath or work with a needle when there was a thunderstorm heading our way in the good old South-West Africa of forty plus years ago - how times flies. The pregnant smell of waiting dust, the earsplitting silence before the first crack, then the sound of fat drops breaking the waiting earth and the uncontrollable outpour of joy when the skies clear with people shouting, dogs barking and children running, often naked through the muddy brown curling fast flowing waters of the Okahandja River.

The good old days, a bit like the current good Irish days except for the dust and the barking dogs. Even dogs are civil in this place and wheelie bins don't fall over. It can be so boring.

This place is still very much off the beaten track, still protected by Her Majesty and the Irish still so stubborn that it will make any real Afrikaner proud.

Talk about taking the good but spiting out everything else. And I am the heaviest that I have ever been. Time for me to start spitting things out or not opening my mouth in the first place.

Thought I was heavy when it dawned on me that I was the heaviest in the queue to get skis two years ago during our skiing trip to Italy. It was like being on a conveyer belt: getting kitted out with rented skis, goggles, jackets, etc and you had to shout your weight to the guy setting the tension on the skis! 105 and a bit kilograms were met with silence and it was a clear day with the sun blinding on the bright virgin snow. This time round I may have to use two smallish fishing boats. (I mean: a few kilograms over 105 is nothing - that is like the potatoes that a healthy Irish farmer will eat in a week!) But then, that was two years ago and this is the land of milk and honey and potato and chilli cream chicken and meat and a wee Irish woman, so the few is now a lot.

We are seriously thinking / planning a Southern Africa trip towards the end of Oct 2010. The idea is to do even more and see even more than last time.

Flying into JHB, driving via Botswana (Gaborone) and

Namibia (Kasane) to Cape Town and flying back home. All in less than three weeks and on a limited budget. It may be a bit too much to bite off, but still very much at planning stage and may well change.

It is becoming more and more expensive and I would love Linda to see some of Botswana (she loved the "*1st Lady Detective books*" - Google it), the Vic falls, experience a bit of the Okavango Delta, Etosha, Swakop, Okahandja, the Fish River and I have to see Werner, Michael, Marinette and Ty before the year is out or die from a broken heart!

So anybody that has done a similar trip is welcome to flood my inbox.

Take care and only open your mouth when it is safe to do so.

"Out of Africa" - one of Linda's all-time favorite movies.
Living with dementia - an eye opener.
What are we but our memories?
What are we when thoughts of the past awaken ghosts of the future?

I am a wee bit home sick, so planning the upcoming trip to Southern Africa gives me something to look forward too, but it also brings the big practical problem of care for Linda's mom while we are away and in a way forces one to face ones own demons, especially now that one of my younger South African friends has had a heart attack.

The old lady was 80 a week or so ago (I can't remember exactly when) and has the short term memory of a burned out match. She! Not me!!

It will be four years on the 26th of October since I first set food in Ireland – both South (The Republic of Ireland) and North (the Ireland that is part of the UK). Ireland is not a very big place.

Back to the future: I think the other sister and brother may be somewhat "reluctant" to sleep over to look after her (who can blame them?) and she doesn't "like" Adam, Linda's only son to sleep over even when we are not around as he "lifts" her earrings (but then only the odd single one), pineapple, hairspray, chocolates and then not for his own use, but for his pretty wee 21 year old girlfriend.

They, Adam and Cara, are moving to Manchester in the next month or so - both have graduated a few weeks ago from Queens University in Belfast and Adam is starting with DeLoyds while Cara is a personal trainer at a gym even though she graduated with a degree in English - strange indeed.

But back to taking stuff: the 80 year old old-Lady used to care for Adam when he was a wee little boy and Linda had to go on business trips to aforementioned Manchester. He, Adam is the best Grandson ever.

Anyway, the solution is easy: She, the 80 year old old-Lady, hides everything that she likes when Adam is at home or when she thinks he will be coming home or may be at home, even when he isn't - ours is not to reason why. That includes the above mentioned personal treasures plus a few other odds and ends just to be sure to be sure. Preferably perishables like fruit, sugary biscuits (or "buns" as it is called here in Ireland - both north and south) and chocolates.

You know, things that one only finds when it either explodes or starts crawling by itself! But I have discovered a few secret hiding places to search just to be sure to be sure: the bottom of the dirty washing basket in the hot-press, behind the pullout drawer under her double bed or behind the heavy headboard, behind the cane vegetable drawer in the kitchen and then on top of the kitchen cupboards.

How does a five foot one inch eighty year old old-Lady manage to hide two two-for-£3.00 vacuum sealed packets of Tesco pineapple slices on top of build-in solid light stained oak kitchen units? If only she could remember!

Interesting indeed and who knows, it may be laying in wait for all of us!

She tends to doze during the day to wake one in the dead of night looking for her handbag, a meal, a wee cup of tea, to tell you that she is diabetic and has to eat now, that she needs exactly £1.35 for her lunch at the centre that she attends three times a week (Mondays, Wednesdays & Fridays), looking for the dog that is snoring on her bed, to ask whether you have *"lifted"* her pension from the Post Office (I am so impressed by the service of Royal Mail but that is another story all together), what day it is, to count her money, to ask whether she has taken her tablets or to say that she is not going to take a bath.

Very interesting as she may ask / say / do the same thing four times in three minutes. And then again. And she has rhymes to recite to prompt her memory once you have jump started it! Interesting.
"What day is it?" Clear as a silver tea bell on a white serviette with butlers on hand, standing upright, hair neat in curlers next to your bed.
"Tuesday morning half two." cloudy from under the duvet. (It took me ages to get round this half two, half three thing - the Brits are different.)
"Monday, Wednesday, Friday is when I go to the Meadows! Where do I go Tuesdays?"
Or *"What time does the bus come to pick me up"* if it should be Monday, Wednesday or Friday.

Very interesting as The Bible would say - the flight of a bird, something else and the ways of a woman's heart. Nothing about dementia though!

201

Don't get me wrong! She is as fit as they come and can touch the floor with flat hands without bending her knees. She makes her own bed, brushes the dog. She knows everybody's telephone number by heart. She uses sugar pills in her tea as she is diabetic but will not touch a cup of tea if not accompanied by something sweet to eat and to share with the dog. She "smoothes" (irons) the smaller square things like hankies and she has the singing voice of an Angel. She loves me to bits and will wake me in the middle of the night to give me a few sweets on a white paper serviette. Sweets that she gets when going to the pictures on a Saturday night - has not missed it in the three years that I have known her.

Plus - she phones the boyfriend (Tom 88 and brighter than any 57 year old) to come and pick her up as she has been stuck in the house the whole day - that as you trip over her while carrying the bags into the house after a six hour family shopping trip that included three cups of tea and sugary buns! The same 88 year old old-gentleman that takes her to the pictures every Saturday and buys the sweets. Tom that doesn't wear glasses and still works at his trade as an electrician at a chicken farm. Tom that fixed the new light fittings in the hallway that I left for later after blowing the fuse...

They don't pay for the cinema tickets or the complimentary cup of tea and bun. The two old Dears are to be behold. I often wonder what they are up to in the back seats of the cinema and why they will park outside the house for hours before she enters with a song and a smile?

"Anybody at home?"

Questions, questions everywhere and not a drop to drink. That is the way of life - I was 58 today a week ago.

Tomorrow is the 1st of September; start of Spring in South Africa but not here, this side of the world. So I went out to celebrate the arrival of Autumn in the northern Hemisphere.

I went out today at lunchtime, all by my lonesome self and had a leisurely hour long walk and a Nando's Chicken Burger (Double, Lemon & Herb +Cheese +Pine with one side of regular chips) and a soft drink - bottom line £12.35.

I took the long way round to get to Victoria Square & Nando's flagship shop in the centre of Belfast, Northern Ireland. It is a really beautiful warm (18+ degree) cloudless windless day with lots of tourists hanging about. Nature in all her glory, a miracle indeed. Isn't life great. Isn't the gift of life just so... so really fantastic?

Really strange - these tourists. Millions of them (even though the Australian minister of tourism has warned Ausies from visiting Northern Ireland at the moment due to all the bombs and flare-up of *The Troubles*).

The Troubles in Northern Ireland means something different to troubles at home, but is sort of the same thing - fight with those that you love and live with. A lot like the Afrikaners, people in touch with their inner feelings and not afraid to beat it into others that may disagree.

I also bought a torch on the spur of the moment at one of those man shops that have circular saws in the window - a precision engineered aluminium body and rubber switch weather resistant extra large security torch. Talking about torches: one is not allowed to carry anything that may vaguely resemble a weapon. Definitely no traditional weapons allowed, but Zulus welcome. Not even a Swiss pocket knife. So taxi drivers and the like keep these long heavy-duty steel reinforced torches in their cars - for light you see.

Anyway, I have seen the light.
It will be three years tomorrow since I have first laid eyes on the wee Irish Sunshine Girl.

I have also watched an interesting TV program presented by the man that wrote the God Delusion, professor Richard Dawkins.

Linda works these strange long 14+ hour shifts and that gives me time to catch-up on the odd TV documentary while the old lady is out with her boy Tom. Tom that is 88 and his newly broken tooth. He was trimming his hedges last week and a branch knocked out the one front tooth, but not-to-worry. NHS may just replace it before he gets his letter from the Queen in twelve years' time.

Tom who played cricket for Ireland many years ago before the time of planned no-balls. He also played soccer for one of the local clubs; still have oats every morning seven days a week and a three course meal that includes pudding every evening - all cooked by him and with spuds and lots of real Irish butter.

So I watch TV rather than trimming the hedge or cutting the grass or washing the car or sleeping or emailing the people in Sunny South Africa. (It is not as if I ever get any replies to my emails, you know.)

Anyway, why does he care? Richard Dawkins that is. "Let them stew in their own religious juices", I shouted at the TV.

My poor stomach can't handle Nando's mild, hot or extra hot anymore and that is why I had the Lemon & Herb! I do however still find the never ending never winning religious debates rather interesting old chap, even though I have realised some time ago that religion and doctors are to be ignored for a better, longer and more rewarding existence!

Tom even grows his own veggies, including tomatoes. So many tomatoes that I can't stay ahead - two sliced fresh tomatoes on toast with lots of salt and black pepper makes for a really nice TV snack.

So I walked passed the Belfast Fish and all the tourists that it has caught. Smiling people hanging over the walls next to the river, open mouth people listening to the tour guide telling them about the dead concrete fish covered with lots of different size mainly pale blue broken tiles. The fish is right next to the gateway to the Titanic Tours head quarters.

There must be something in it and I don't mean Jonah - it is a solid fish that has never seen water. And I thought, who else but the proud stubborn god-fearing Irish can spin a national engineering disaster like the sinking of the Titanic into a moneymaking racket that attracts people from all over the world, even Australia?

As Richard Dawkins quoted: *"It takes religion to make good people do bad things"*.

I am also bored out of my tree when Linda is not around. TG, the Sunday shift is behind us the next four weeks!

It is a dark and stormy night.
Well, not quite.
It is however a grey and wet and very Irish Autumn day. We are still in summer time and that is the only thing summer about this grey wet Irish Friday!

It is dark, it is wet and a wee bit cold, but I guess just because my clothes are still a wee bit damp after I went out (4 hours ago) to lift a wee cup of coffee and a toasty of sausage and bacon on brown bread with tomato relish. Freshly made and only £2.95, but then only if bought before 12 o'clock.

Pleasant young Polish girl that runs the O'Brien shop where I get my morning take-out coffee. Girl all alone and it does get busy, especially when only ducks and the Irish will venture outside (and the odd older more mature WAM).

And I do have variety in my life (and I don't mean women)! For breakfast I rotate between O'Briens and Carberry. O'Briends with coffee and a toasty for £2.95 and Carberry with coffee and porridge for £3.55. Porridge equals Oats. No "mieliepap" here - what a pity!

I have a different routine for lunchtime, but not now. Enough to say that it involves a walk and a chemist. I am still busy with the grey wet Irish morning and the 1st of October 2010.

I start work before the rest of the population wakes up.

I get up before the rest of the population goes to bed.

May as it is, it is way too early to even think of breakfast. I normally switch the office lights on any time between 07:00 & 07:30, drop my wet windbreaker, scan my emails and then go out for a wee coffee and a breakfast toasty of sausage & bacon on brown with tomato relish or coffee and a bowl of oats. This takes my 20 year old Omega Constellation (same age as the wee Polish girl) to anywhere between 08:30 and 09:00 (depending on number of emails) - still a few minutes of "*me-time*" before the rest of the team will shiver in.

Did you people see the news about Sidy Sidy Sidy Nomis and his leg? The flying Jewish boy's leg was amputated! What a pity!

Today is the 1st of October - *die mooiste mooiste maand.*

"Dit is die maand Oktober! Die mooiste, mooiste maand! Dan is die dag so helder, so groen is elke aand, so blou en sonder wolke die hemel heerlik bo, so blomtuin vol van kleure die asvaal ou Karoo, so blomtuin vol van kleure die asvaal ou Karoo.

Dit is die maand Oktober! Die varkblom is in bloei; oor al die seekoeigate is "blomme" gegroei; die koppies, kort gelede nog as 'n klip so kaal, het nou vir welkomsgroetnis hul mooiste voor gehaal; het nou vir welkomsgroetnis hul mooiste voor gehaal.

Dit is die maand Oktober! Die akkerboom is groen; die bloekoms langs die paaie is almal nuut geboen; en orals in die tuin rond ruik jy sering en roos, jasmyn en katjiepiering, lemoen en appelkoos, jasmyn en katjiepiering, lemoen en appelkoos.

208

Dit is die maand Oktober! Ek dink die mense vier vir ewig in die hemel Oktobermaand soos hier! Wat wens jy meer as blomme, as helder dag en nag? Wat kan jy beter, mooier of heerliker verwag? Wat kan jy beter, mooier of heerliker verwag?

Wat gee ek om die winter? Wat praat jy nou van Mei? Wat skeel dit as ons later weer donker dae kry? Ek is nou in Oktober, die mooiste, mooiste maand, met elke dag so helder, so pragtig elke aand! Met elke dag so helder, so pragtig elke aand!"

Let's just hope heaven is not an eternity of Irish Octobers!

You know, the old story of "*sometimes I sit and think and sometimes I just sit*"?
Or to quote Fanus "*Van sit en staan is lê die lekkerste*"?

But thinking or not and standing or no: I have made a wee discovery.
I may just die one day.
Strange thought I know, but I guess not too many people do actually realise that and therefore give it any thought.

Even stranger that a few people I know, have died lately.
People younger and fitter than me.

I hope people have a good laugh with me when I die.
That is what I think; when I think.
A good laugh and a sort of knowingly shaking of the head, (may you all be grey by then).

Come to think of it: it will be real interesting - this running into a wall that will not give way and then nothing. Really interesting - worth thinking about sometimes when you just sit or when you wake up at 2 o'clock in the morning with the sleeping house reassuringly breathing around you through its creaking joints and your whole world a cozy bed.

So remember, a good friendly warm laugh: not too loud and maybe just a few silent red eye nearly tears. That is what I will appreciate. Damming tears behind red walls like when you watch something on TV and you don't want that special person next to you to know that now is not the right time to ask a question, as there is a wee something in your throat / heart / eye. That will be good when I run into the black darkness, so don't forget:

Remember me when I am gone away,
Gone far away into the silent land;
When you can no more hold me by the hand,
Nor I half turn to go yet turning stay.
Remember me when no more day by day
You tell me of our future that you plann'd:
Only remember me; you understand
It will be late to counsel then or pray.
Yet if you should forget me for a while
And afterwards remember, do not grieve:
For if the darkness and corruption leave
A vestige of the thoughts that once I had,
Better by far you should forget and smile
Than that you should remember and be sad.

Christina Rossetti

My advice?

Have a good life.
It is the only one you will ever have.
This is the real thing
not a dress rehearsal.

So go out
and spend some money.
It is not real - it is man printed
and, like man, here today and worthless tomorrow.

212

So spread it around.
It is not going to keep you warm or cozy when others have
 to go without...

TG I am not a Christian / Hindu / Maya / Muslim...
That will make dying real hard and not at all interesting.

Not being afraid makes life real interesting.
I think, when I think, that I have another thirty years of
interest in me...

From: Johann Wentzel
Sent: Wed 08/12/2010 16:28
63. Subject: No, I don't know but

I don't know how deep the snow is at our little village named Waringstown next to Lurgan about 20 miles or so from Belfast, the capital of Northern Ireland. I guess I can measure Tyro's legs (Tyro is the dog) and then tell how deep the snow is at our little village called Waringstown next to Lurgan etc etc etc.

Quite simple - I have started taking Tyro for a walk now that we have snow and he enjoys it. So do I. We walk at night around eight o'clock and if nobody looks, melt wee yellow flowers in the white snow. And his, Tyro's stomach brushes the snow. It is also not possible to tell where the pavement ends and where the road begins when walking around our estate; an estate is like a complex without gates and armed guards and fences with lots of Christmas decorations and children's bicycles & toys hidden under the snow. All things hidden that Tyro has to inspect and approve with his own unique smell.

I normally start the walk armed with three plastic Tesco bags to collect his more permanent markers. I also tend to repeat an Afrikaans word reinforced by the DISTRICT 9 DVD when he chooses to leave a message right in front of people's doors while they are watching.

Did you watch District 9? I thoroughly enjoyed it, especially the remark / scene about the "prawns popping" when the shack was set alight! But back to our pretty snow-white little village Waringstown next to Lurgan...

Snow is pretty loose fluffy white stuff that crunches when you drive over it. It then becomes all dark and gloomy and muddy, so much so that you have to sweep the garage when you take the car out to go to work in the dark. That is any time between half six and seven in the morning - long before anybody else.

The dark gloomy muddy snow cakes do not melt so there is no rush. I usually sweep it out in the evening before parking the car for the night. I mean, I sweep out yesterday's dark gloomy snow mud cakes tonight before depositing tonight's to be swept out tomorrow evening - I am well organised.

We, Linda and I are two of the few that park cars in the garage and only because I have repacked the garage. The rest of the population (99,9%) uses garages to store Christmas presents I guess - not children's bicycles or toys for sure, and leave their cars outside. So they have to defrost windows before they can go to work, to friends, the bus stop, the shops, the doctor, for a drive. Sometimes they can't even open their car doors. Anyway, so they will eventually get the windscreen etc cleared of the now melted snow that has turned into frozen sticky clinging ice, open the door and start the car and then close the door before going back into the warm cozy picture pretty house covered in pretty lose fluffy white snow, for breakfast / coffee / the toilet while the car heats up. All very well planned and organised.

It is really pretty and not that cold - it takes Tyro about ten minutes to run out of yellow snow paint. I run out much sooner if nobody is watching. (It also takes me about ten minutes to lose the feelings in my hand holding the lease, and my ears.)

Good thing I grew up in Africa so have lots of creative ideas. Not like the lot here that must be told to do things or not to do things. Like being told that snow may turn into ice and that ice may be slippery. That you may even fall when walking on ice that used to be snow. That you must make sure that you have petrol in your car before driving from Waringstown to Belfast - all 20 miles. That you must have at least one warm meal a day and not only drink. That you must switch your Christmas lights on / off. That you are not allowed to use the plug that came with your Christmas lights if it doesn't have a fuse in the actual plug (Elbereth's English boyfriend wanted to call an electrician to change their plug but luckily Elbereth told him to do it himself. Luckily she could show him how to do it.) They may well be moving to South Africa early in the New Year. He may even survive a few days if he doesn't cross the road, eat a cold meal, use a car, go out of the house, run a bath, try and cook something, plug in the TV.

It is quite strange, come to think of it. Cars here stop when you put your foot off the pavement to cross the road even if you don't know where the pavement ends and the road starts. Flashing lights mean you are welcome to cut or walk in front of me and NOT get the hell out of the way.

Really strange and pretty white wee island this, with its forty shades of green when not covered in snow as it has been the last week or is that two?

Also still lots and lots to eat - especially now with Christmas just weeks away. But then, we should not call it Christmas, should we? It may just upset people that don't celebrate Christmas (I still have to meet one) so we call it something else. I am not giving the secret away - come and visit during the festive season and experience the joys for yourself.

It is more that seven and a half inches - I measured it when nobody was looking, but then it was cold so I may be wrong!

Just open and scroll down to see some of the pretty white pictures!
http://www.dailymail.co.uk/news/article-1336705/Britain-shivers-fresh-snowfalls-blizzards-head-south.html

From: Johann Wentzel
Sent: Mon 31/01/2011 17:01
64. **Subject:** Hot of the press! Act now, don't delay

Friends and others.

My "memoirs" (times 2 actually) are available and may be ordered directly from the publishers.

But first, for my non-South African friends (and others).
tickey ['tiki]
n
(Historical Terms) a South African threepenny piece, which was replaced by the five-cent coin in 1961
[of uncertain origin]
Collins English Dictionary – Complete and Unabridged © HarperCollins Publishers 1991, 1994, 1998, 2000, 2003

It was written in Afrikaans and I must admit, it was not easy to translate into the Queen's language, but read for yourself! It may just raise a laugh and hopefully a few tears.

For orders:
Illette Strydom at Groep7drukkers
Her (Illete's) cellphone / mobile is +27 82 4490 574.
Email epos@groep7.co.za

Or "Google" it.

Or speak to me!

Book 1:

Where is my tickey? *A journey through my youth.*

Life is good to me... I am a child of Namibia.
And I know everything...
*   Why there is nothing holy about the tap water of Okahandja.*
*   Why Marinette and I had to turn back.*
*   The Ancient Sun had to die.*
*   Bushmen trek when it rains in the desert.*
*   It is better to pass away than to die.*
*   There is too little god.*
*   Why there are still kudu left in Namibia.*
*   A little dust was raised on the moon.*
*   My year in the defence force was a good one.*
*   Why I buy only the softest double-layered white toilet paper*
*   and not eat apricot jam*
*   Where to find that little secret hole...*

What I did not know and only realised when I was almost fifty
years old, is that we were poor.

Lariza van Niekerk:
It is enjoyable and relaxing to read "Where is my tickey",
which is always the best criterion. I do not want to struggle
through something that I read... one struggles enough in life!
The stories are interesting, and I like the way two parallel
storylines usually develop in one narrative. It captivates one's
attention. The language usage is natural and suits the type of
narratives. The result is a snug fireside book to read, not only
for the author's family and friends, but for anyone interested in
delighting in this type of literature.

Book 2:

I have found my Tickey.

Rejoice with me,
I have found my tickey.
Plus
   two brothers and a sister
   a son and two daughters
   more than one wife...

Actually, my tickey has always been there:
   together on the long road,
   with the inquisitive discovery of all ten secret holes,
   the 'naked hikers',
   with the birth of my children,
   the death of my parents, my brother, my son
   my own journey back, always back...
   I am a child of Namibia.

Lariza van Niekerk:
What a pleasure it is to go on a reminiscence journey with Johann Wentzel in "I have found my Tickey"! This journey stretches from his barefoot childhood days in South-West Africa and South Africa to Northern Ireland, from curry-tripe In Okahandja to curry-chips in Letterkenny. With the author, we have the honour of a near royal reception at a wedding in Taung, to be intrigued by the medicine man's fresh goat-skin apron and eventually to find true happiness in Waringstown. The narratives are presented in a casual style and that captivates the reader and lets the reader join the visit.

From: Johann Wentzel
Sent: Wed 15/12/2010 11:44
65. Subject: Werner Wentzel - 20 Nov 1974 to 15 Dec 2010

My son Werner passed away in his sleep early this morning - December 15. Werner was severely disabled and cared for in a care-home called Vita Nova just outside Johannesburg, South Africa. http://web.eject.co.za/vitanova/about.htm

I will not be going to South Africa, but the immediate family will have a private memorial service in Oxted, Surrey (UK) on the 28th of December. Werner's mom Anne-Marie, sister Marinette, her husband Michael and wee Ty are scheduled to arrive in London this Saturday, Dec 18.

Werner and I:

223

Werner will be cremated and we will scatter his ashes when I next visit South Africa - hopefully Easter 2011

For family and friends.
We will appreciate donations to Vita Nova rather than flowers.

For more information re Vita Nova please feel free to contact them.

Many thanks / Baie dankie.

From: Johann Wentzel
Sent: Wed 05/01/2011 14:43
66. Subject: Get your dress made - we are flying Friday the 25th of March and will be back Sunday the 3rd of April!

This is so exciting!

PS - Don't tell anybody you pretty wee bride!

From: Johann Wentzel
Sent: Wed 05/01/2011 16:50
67. Subject: To the Bride-to-Be from the lucky (if not always silent) Man!

My Dearie.

If you will do me the honor and arrive in your wee pretty dress, with a blush on your face, barefoot on the beach of the Shandrani Resort, Mauritius on the 2nd of April 2011 to make this, sometimes quite man really really happy. (He does not mind waiting the whole day - you may take your time.)

To facilitate this, this man (that is me) will make sure that you, plus this man (still me) will be on the plane for Mauritius on Saturday the 26th of March 2011 and that this man (hopefully still me) will deliver you back in Northern Ireland in one "peice" on Tuesday, the 5th of April 2011 as Mrs. Linda Joyce Cunningham Wentzel.

This man (whether you come back with him or not) also promises to make sure that you will not go hungry or thirsty during this island adventure.

That this man will further endeavour to secure a room on the ground floor with an ocean view for the duration of the stay at said resort.

That all questions that you may have will be answered in due course.

That the cost of said life-changing experience comes to a total of just over £x,xxx.xx but less than £x,xxx.xx, which costs include the return flights from Dublin via Paris to Mauritius and accommodation at the Shandrani Resort on a 08 nights hotel all inclusive + wedding package basis, but not wedding photos.

For further information re the resort:
http://www.dreamweddings.co.uk/hotel/indian-ocean/mauritius/216-shandrani-resort-amp-spa

For further information and a practical introduction re the Lucky Man, just ask me!

The wedding vows

I Wynand Johannes Wentzel, take you, Linda Joyce Boyd, to be my wife, my partner in life and my one true love.

I will cherish our union and love you more each day than I did before.

I will trust you and respect you, laugh with you and cry with you, loving you faithfully through good times and bad, regardless of the obstacles we face together.

I give you my hand, my heart, and my love, from this day forward for as long as we both shall live.

Mauritius - 2 April 2011

A Story for Linda

I was born on the 24th of August 1952. I had another birth experience fifty five years and one day later. Don't forget the one day.

I did not want to be born on that Sunday, that Sunday of the 24th of August 1952. I did not like the dust and the heat, but mainly the dust. There were dust-devils swirling around outside: I could see it through the opening in the corner of the bedroom where my Mother was struggling to convince me otherwise. It was a house constructed mainly from corrugated iron sheets.

I arrived just after sunset - in the windless quite born by the late Sunday dusk. My mother was eighteen years old. She was in labour for over eighteen hours. I may still carry the scars. I was my Mother's blue eye boy.

It was the Friday evening after my fifty-fifth birthday. I was at peace with the world and the world at peace with me. There was no wind blowing outside. There was definitely no dust. It was a mild August Friday evening in Northern Ireland.

There are no dust storms in Northern Ireland. Not even when the farmers bring out their tractors to plough the fields waiting for the potatoes - Queens and Pinks. I was home alone.

I was born in a town called Odendaalsrus. It is more like a village slap bang at the centre of the Gold Fields of the

Orange Free State, one of the four official provinces of Republic of South Africa. Odendaalsrus is about five miles from Welkom, the sometimes unofficial capital of the Gold Fields.

My parents used to move house and provinces quite a lot. I attended a number of primary schools and three high schools spread over three provinces. Namibia was regarded as the fifth province of the Republic of South Africa in those days. The world was less complicated then.

I am the eldest of four children, three boys and a girl.
It's my Mother's birthday the day after Christmas, the 26th of December. I was born at the right time.

Bready is a wee village about eight miles north (or is that south?) of Londonderry (or is that Derry?). It is also about eighty miles from Waringstown where the sun lives. Certain things we just know.

My one brother was born in the Free State as well but in a place called Bethel, not Bethlehem. My sister was born in Okahandja, a town in Namibia forty five miles north of Windhoek: Windhoek being the official capital of Namibia. Namibia was still called South-West Africa in those days. My baby brother, nearly eleven years younger than me, was born in Windhoek. Windhoek was where I started high school.

One can smell the liquid fertilizer that the potato farmers spray over their lands. It smells like manure, no doubt about that and will hang in the air for days on end, a bit like the dust storms hanging over the Orange Free State when the fields are ploughed to prepare it for the mealies. Vast dusty fields that will not always born a crop due to the lack of follow-up rains during the planting season.

The liquid fertilizer is transported by narrow winding BaBa Black Sheep roads in tanks pulled by tractors that make you want to be a boy again. Bright red (Ferguson) and green (John Deer) tractors toying with tanks running on balloon tyres in and out of water lodged fields.

I moved to Northern Ireland at the right time in my life.
It is Linda's birthday on the 30th of March.

My Sunshine Girl

The gods sometimes punish us by bestowing upon us that what we pray for; a bit like the honey pot in Pharaohs tomb.

I was fifty five years and one day old: don't forget the one day, when the gods smiled upon me. They have not turned their faces away since. Neither has she, the Sunshine Girl – my little Sunshine Girl. That was August 25, 2007. My birthday is on the 24th of August - every year. I am a Virgo, but thank the gods, only by the stars.

My parents gave me a Pentax MS SLR camera for my 21st birthday. I sold it a few years later. That was after Werner, my only son was born: Sold to keep the wolf at bay. That however, is another story. Anne-Marie bought me the later module years later: long after I have stopped attempting to develop and print my own photos. I still have that camera. I also fathered two beautiful daughters.

Anyway, my sister Monica is my junior by four-and-a-bit years. I once made her sit on an old iron garden chair. Actually more like balancing on the back of the steel frame chicken wire covered chair with her feed on the chair's white coated seat to get the lighting just right and took a photo of her face: A face not looking directly at the camera but rather scanning the unseen future horizons. I then superimposed this into (or is that onto?) the photo image of an upturned lid of a pottery jar from my Mother's kitchen. The end result was quite good for someone so young and impatient: too impatient to wait for the developing process to run its proper course: A golden disk that trapped my sister's nearly seventeen year old face forever. A bit like the baby preserved in the honey. It is boring working in a darkroom.

Funny things, birthdays: They come and they go. They are also markers, milestones along our individual journeys. Resting places along a road that may be lonesome at times even when you are with people: More so when you get older. We all need sunshine along the way. I replied to 59Lady. Friday evenings are good for taking checkpoints.

I also have a photo of my brother, flat on his back laying on the lawn in front of my parents' house. A close up of his side profile, head only - balancing an apple in (or is that on?) his open and laughing mouth. My brother is blessed with very good and straight white teeth. He was laughing while keeping his mouth open, balancing the apple. I am two years older than my brother. We both still have our own teeth. Sharks and I leave the same imprint on apples.

It was a Friday evening, the day after my fifty-fifth birthday. I am not one for parties or pubs, have never been. Not even on a Friday: Especially not on a Friday evening after a week of coding away behind a computer keyboard ignoring ringing phones. Friday evenings are the never ending start of recharging the soul, restoring the balance and what better way than pouring your soul into an email. It is also tradition in some communities to eat fish on Fridays.

My sun arrived (or is that arisen?) a week later, not on a Sunday but on a Friday. Her face was not superimposed in a golden lid; it was surrounded by a bit of a haze and carried a *catch-me* smile. I was finally caught barely 24 hours later. It is a sun face that laughs the clouds away. She took the bait. I had an unfair advantage standing high on the pavement when she stopped her car.

The internet is a funny old animal. So is entrusting it with your secrets. It is a bit like fishing. Not the right idea to make your intentions too obvious, but then I was just testing the waters. Not ready to catch or to be caught. There is a place and a time for everything. I arrived at her place a week later: unannounced on a Friday evening. I am impulsive at times, most of the time. I will never grow up; I will only grow old – but not quite yet. Still a lot of spawning left in me. That next day, the Saturday marked the official start of the first day of Spring in South Africa: the country in the sun under the Southern Cross. I cannot recall whether we had fish on that first Friday. I cannot recall much of that first Friday. The Southern Cross consists of five stars.

I bought myself a Pentax digital camera sometime around my fiftieth birthday. It may have been my forty-ninth. Money was not really an object but I did put a lot of research into it: what make to buy, how many pixels, shutter speed, aperture – that sort of thing; the normal process that men go through and I then bought a black one. I always had a thing for black electronic gadgets; black and not manufactured from mainly modern day throw away plastic. It must be a metal frame – and black. I like solid bodies, bodies that don't mind being touched.

I got a black IPod that Christmas – the Christmas of 2007. It was also my second Christmas in Northern Ireland, exactly four months to the day after receiving an answer to my fishing email. The gods and "plenty-of-fish" were good to me. I only had to reply to the reply: Getting my toe into the water. The angel must have been stirring the electronic highway if not the water.

Her Mom was in the car with her when she came to meet me. I ran out of road less than a mile from her house. That was after more than three hours and nearly a hundred miles of previously uncharted territory – there are dragons there. I admitted defeat and phoned for directions. I do not believe in turning around when you get lost. The road is ever ahead of us. I can honestly only recall one time when I had to make a u-turn. That was when I ended up while exploring Inch Island off the road to Buncrana. It was an impulsive detour and the sun was shining. I ended up against the water. Not even I can make a car made of steel travel over water, but I was tempted. There was a salmon farm about 400 meters offshore. A farm that later suffered a million pound sterling disaster when the salmon was killed off by jellyfish. The salmon could not escape their natural enemy due to the constrains of the man made borders that encircled on them. Northern Ireland must be the most beautiful country in the world.

There was also a black Nintendo game console in my Christmas stocking that year. I have the mental age of a twenty four year old. It took me just a few attempts to beat the computer at its own game. I also skied for the first time at fifty five. My Wild Irish Girl is a red slope skier of some experience, experience not limited to only skiing.

I seem to have a slight problem with direction since moving to new shores nearly two years ago. Getting confused between north and south – it must be a change in hemisphere thing, like the water spinning in the wrong

238

direction when you pull the plug in your bath. My Sunshine Girl sometimes says "left" when she really means "right" – a woman thing even in these times of political correctness. I love her for being all woman.

The Foyle River in county Londonderry is the biggest salmon spawning river in the world. Salmon will return year after year to lay their eggs: A journey of some hardship that must not only be undertaken, but a journey that must be completed to ensure the survival of the species. Certain questions need not be asked nor answered. Some journeys start even before we are born. Sometimes we must just be. Northern Ireland is the rest under my foot.

Honey is a gift from the gods, the only food that does not go bad: good enough to preserve a Pharaohs unborn baby. A road travelled in the company of the sun must be the gods' ultimate gift. I am indeed blessed even if we may get lost due to the lack of true north or then left and right. It took me fifty five years and one day to come home – don't forget the one day. We are all cattle of Ra, created from his sweat. It takes Ra one day to complete his never ending journey.

A Funny story for Linda
(A Snow Story)

So, the Eskimos have a whole vocabulary just to describe snow.

Surprise! Surprised? Why am I not surprised!?

I have my own vocabulary for describing snow - solid, rock-solid and rib-shattering-rock-solid to list but a few and that is only on the blue slopes.

Who said white men can't jump or rather white Afrikaner males can't ski? O Lord, it's hard to be humble can not only be claimed by Muhammad Ali, alias Cassius Clay. I may just also change my name - the "*Flying Afrikaner*" skies to mind.

But then, I did not "*dance like a butterfly*".
As for "*sting like a bee*"?
Well, the rib-shattering-rock-solid blue 'snow' did sting and still does and will for another few weeks as per the friendly local safely back-at-home Northern Ireland doctor.

Will I try it again?

Of course: just wait for my ribs to set, my left wrist to carry the weight of a wristwatch again, Craig's goggles replaced and I will queue (once again) to get my Schengen VISA updated - poor Sunshine Girl. But then: it is all her fault.

It all started when she, the one and only Golden Sunshine Girl started the snowball rolling all those many moons ago.

241

It started the day after my fifty-fifth birthday - "*Be warned - I am a skier*" or words to that effect, no photo attached.

For your precious love I will climb the highest mountain
I will even go as far as trying to swim the deepest sea.

Nothing about screaming your head off while hurling down an 85 degree incline covered in rib-shattering-rock-solid white stuff, just to be overtaken by mad men (and women mind you, as I later discovered) dressed in funny baggy patch-painted trousers glued to ironing boards, scrapping the last remaining softer landing spots bare of any hope.

Nothing about spit, snot and tears freezing in streaks to your cheeks.

Nothing about the pain of forcing your angle into a boot that can't bend times two.

Nothing about walking miles and miles with boats strapped to your feet.

Nothing about being dragged off these very same boats by a F1 lollipop trusted into your crutch with such force that it makes your eyes water.

Have you ever tried wiping your eyes behind ski goggles and saving the jewels - all with hands bandaged in layers of padded gloves while, at the same time folding your legs around a witch's broom stick as if you haven't seen a toilet for 36 hours?

And above all, nothing about the embarrassment inflicted by

242

little cozy stuffed three and four years old Jacks-in-boxes manoeuvring themselves in perfect snakelike harmony, little arms solemnly stretched out at a perfect ninety degrees, around your bruised frozen hyperventilating body.

Am I finally admitting to old age silently creaking up?

Not a change!
Far from it - I went, I saw and I conquered: All in six two-hour lessons.

And it was fun, fun and more fun and the company was not too bad either.

And it was in Italy - I have a Schengen VISA plus an Italian entry / exit stamp in my South African passport to proof: That, in addition to the friendly doctor's sworn affidavit.

And will I do it again?
For her - I am willing to sacrifice a rib and throw in a wrist.

"Vonkpos uit Ierland"

From: Johann Wentzel
Sent: Tue 01/08/2006 09:40
68. Subject: Johann W – Ierland

Haai julle klomp daar aan die ander kant van die wêreld.

Dit is nou 4-uur in die oggend, Dinsdag 1 Augustus 2006 en die idee is dat julle almal net my kontakbesonderhede kry en sien dat ek nog lewe. Het so 2-uur opgestaan om wasgoed in die wasmasjien te sit en toe kon ek nie weer slaap nie. (Ja-nee, hier werk 'n man self in die huis.)

Nuus:

Must admit that this is a very civil place, very controlled and I am enjoying it. The scenery is really something else. Looks a lot like New Zealand, just the buildings are much older. People not as stiff as the Brits in England...

Te veel, weet nie waar om te begin nie. Was dit (is dit) die moeite werd? Beslis.
Mis die kinders en Joyce die meeste, dan die "worries" oor alles wat onafgehandel agtergebly het in goeie ou Suid-Afrika. Goed soos die huis en my kar wat nog verkoop moet word, ens. ens. ens.

Voel skoon vreemd by verkeersligte – daar is nie bedelaars nie, het my vrekgesukkel om klerehangers te kry. Die apteke verkoop haardroërs en nie die elektriese winkels nie. Mense wag by verkeersirkels (*round-abouts*) om karre van regs af te laat inkom en hier is baie min Afrikaners...

Dit was 'n tawwe week – van totaal oorgewig wees met die

vertrek uit Jan Smuts / JHB International / OR Tambo, en dit nadat ek twee tasse moes agterlos en nadat ek R2 200 plus vir amper 8 kg ekstra gewig betaal het. Moet erken, het oorspronklik teen 91 kg ingeweeg en op die ou end, na seker twee uur se gesukkel, gevlieg met iets soos 76 kg en 'n klomp handbagasie.

Dit was 'n lang trek – 11-uur Dinsdagoggend die 25ste Julie daar weg en eers na 12 Woensdagmiddag by die gastehuis in Londonderry aangekom. Het die oggend so 7-uur in Dublin geland waar iemand van Northbrook Technology my opgetel het en via Belfast, Londonderry toe gebring het. Die "*killer*" was die 5 uur of so se wag op Bahrain lughawe. Die wag vir die aansluiting na Dublin.

Londonderry is 'n pragtige "stad" en ek het 'n moderne "*apartment*" gekry wat soort van oor die stad en rivier uitkyk. Het eers na twee ander plekke ook gaan kyk voordat daar op dié plekkie besluit is. Op die eerste vloer: twee slaapkamers wat elkeen 'n dubbelbed in het, so is redelik groot (kom kuier!), dan 'n ingangsportaal wat eintlik 'n gang is – mens stap in en dan draai jy links na die sitkamer / eetkamer / kombuis (aldrie in een) en regs na die badkamer en "*utility room*". As jy die "*picture*" kan kry. Houtvloere in die gang en sit-/eetkamer. Teëls in die badkamer en kombuis en matte in die res. Baie spieëls en in ligte kleure geverf.

Die "*utility room*" is so 'n-meter-en-'n-bietjie by 'n-meter-en-'n-bietjie en dit is daar waar die gasverwarmer is, plus 'n ingeboude stofsuier wat 'n suigpunt in die gang het – het mos gesê dit is modern! Elke vertrek het sentrale verwarming. Die hoofslaapkamer het groot glasdeure wat op 'n "*bay window*" oopmaak, so ook die sitkamer. Kan egter nie uitstap nie. In elk geval, nou eers genoeg van die huis.

Het gister (Maandag) begin werk. Nuwe gebou wat Oktober 2005 geopen is. Begin op die oomblik 9-uur werk en gaan halfses huis toe – die son is alreeds 5-uur op en gaan eers na tien onder. Werk lyk rustig. Mense egter besig, maar lyk nie of daar baie druk is nie – gewone ou IT-storie egter, "*users*" wat kla omdat dinge lank vat en nie deeglik getoets is nie, ens. Doen werk vir 'n Amerikaanse korttermyn versekeringsmaatskappy. Meeste programme is COBOL en hoofsaaklik "*batch*". *Batch* loop van 6 tot 8 in die oggend. Mengsel van mense: werk saam met iemand van Singapoer, dan 'n klomp mense van Indië en "*locals*". Sukkel baie met almal se aksente – wens die mense het Engels gepraat!

Deel van my voordele is lidmaatskap by 'n "*gym*" wat regs langs die werk is. Die kantoorblok is op die Magee universiteitskampus en ek is binne loopafstand van die werk af. Sal egter op 'n stadium 'n karretjie moet aanskaf. Die taxi-diens is baie goed en redelik geprys! Alle karre ouer as vier jaar moet elke jaar vir 'n toets gaan, so die meeste karre is nuut en almal padwaardig. Versekering is blykbaar redelik hoog, plus mens betaal "*road tax*" wat gebaseer is op die enjingrootte van die kar. Alle verkeersoortredings maak dat jy punte kry en sodra jy 12 punte het, word jou lisensie vir 'n jaar opgeskort. Iets soos sonder 'n veiligheidsgordel ry, is 4 punte, 75 in 'n 60 sone is 3 punte, plus dan nog regte egte geldboetes ook. "Geld" soos in ponde!

Bo-op Londonderry se muur:

Buite die dorp:

Johann Wentzel
Sent: Wed 23/08/2006 12:24
69. Subject: Sommer bietjie nuus

More of the same.
Ek is besig om hierdie plek al meer te geniet - gaan slaap elke aand met pyne in my bene van al die stap. Het nie kompetisie van die mans hier nie - die Ierse mans het rooi hare. Terloops, die aftree-ouderdom in die UK verander blykbaar Oktober na 68 en daar mag nie teen die oues gediskrimineer word nie. Daar is 'n ou van 70 wat saam werk en wat vies is omdat sy aansoek vir 'n verband afgekeer is.

Het ook iets soos "FICA" hier - moet bewys waar jy bly voordat jy kan skuld maak - ek probeer om nie skuld te maak nie, maar ek het toe SKY TV gekry - is verlede Vrydagaand ingesit - wil SA rugby kyk. SKY premium (al die kanale) kos £42-50 'n maand (omtrent dieselfde as DSTV) - eerste drie maande is dit £10-00. Broadband is so £15-00 per maand en telefoonlyn is £11-00. Ons kan in die middag by die universiteit eet - 'n goeie ete daar kos £2-20 of £2-30. In die oggend eet ek *oats*. Kruideniersware is redelik geprys, net die vleis lyk snaaks - baie rooi en pap - glad nie soos 'n Karoo-tjoppie nie. Koop baie *mince* en het al die eerste *stew* in die nuwe *slowcooker* gemaak. Het nog nie 'n plek gekry waar mens *oxtail* kan koop nie.

Mens sukkel ook om uit te werk wat goed kos omdat dit so min klink - 9 rolle toiletpapier vir seker so £2-00 wat R26-00 is. En ek verdien relatief minder in ponde as wat ek in rande verdien het. Lyk darem asof belasting bietjie minder kan wees en die voordele meer. Sal op die ou end 'n kar moet

251

koop - so bietjie minder as £9000-00 vir 'n amper nuwe 2005 Ford Focus LX wat minder as 4000 myl op die klok het. Dis die kar wat ek gehuur het. Kry karre ouer as 4 jaar goedkoper omdat alle karre ouer as 4 jaar elke jaar getoets moet word - sal seker iets kan kry vir so £2500-00 tot £3500-00, dan is die *road tax* en versekering egter hoër. Versekering vir my op die Focus is £428-00 vir 'n jaar. Rentekoers is 6,4 wat beteken die paaiement is £200-00 per maand oor 48 maande. Sal beslis minder as £50 se petrol 'n maand uitry, al ry ek baie. Ierland is klein en mens kan in elk geval nie werk toe ry nie. Hier is egter redelik parkering in die dorp self.

Wat die werk aangaan, Suid-Afrika (Banke / stelsels) ligjare voor. Die stelsels waarop ons werk is egter baie meer stabiel - omtrent geen *callout* nie. Die werkers het baie voordele en daar word gedurig nog dinge bygesit of iets anders genoem. Goed soos *Duvet Leave* - jy mag een dag 'n jaar inbel en sê jy is nie vandag lus vir werk nie. Solank jy net voor tien inbel. Dag gaan dan van jou gewone verlof af. Of jy kan tyd inwerk om tyd af te vat, maar nie meer as een dag in 'n 4 weke-*cycle* nie en ook nie meer as ses dae 'n jaar nie. Kan dit egter in halwe dae opbreek. Mens beheer jou eie verlofvorms en het eers 'n doktersertifikaat nodig na sewe dae weg van die werk af. Vreeslik baie reëls en regulasies. Lyk egter asof mense van hul leefwyse hou, so almal kom die reëls na en doen die ding volgens die boek.

Maar dit gaan lekker hier. Mense moer *nice* and die plek is lig en skoon - loop in die aand langs die rivier (omdat dit daar is waar die meisies draf en glo my, die meisies hier is baie meer om na te kyk as die mans). Hier en daar 'n ou wat kitaarspeel vir 'n geldjie, maar niemand wat bedel nie. Bietjie graffiti op van die mure, maar stap in enige hool in om iets te eet of te drink. As jy nie van 'n plek hou nie, stap jy weer uit. Almal waarsku egter dat dinge drasties anders is in die winter - son wat eers 8-uur op kom en weer 4-uur onder is.

My lewer kla nou eers erg as ek Guinness drink. Drink nou eerder *Cranberry juice*. Oral kry jy water saam met jou ete as jy net vra - sommer 'n beker yswater as jy wil hê. Nou die dag iets soos Oros gekry - gratis en verniet.

Moet baie goed wat die mense hier as vanselfsprekend aanvaar, self doen of laat doen - goed soos by 'n dokter registreer, *national security*-nommers kry, Visa's laat stempel en hoe dinge werk. Vat alles nogal tyd ook, veral omdat ek alles moet herhaal en dan weer die mense moet vra om alles te herhaal, ai tog, die ou Engels.

Was sommer bietjie gesels - groete vir almal daar.

Die weer is fantasties, nat, grys, winderig en lekker.

Lekker *cosy*-slaap-weer terwyl mens dieselfde tyd voel asof jy meer energie het: dit terwyl jy so koes-koes teen die wind, teen die motreën, teen die '*hill*' uit skuifel-skuifel terug na jou warm huis en bed, so skuins gedraai om die bietjie-bietjie nat uit jou gesig te hou en dan so met die skuinsdraai, onder jou kappie te loer na meisies met rooi-van-koue nat lippe, gespan in 'n wit asemwolkie-glimlag. Ai, die winterweer in Ierland is lekker man! En Sondagoggend die 29-ste Oktober, om twee-uur die oggend, kry ons 'n uur by. Moet mens opstaan om jou horlosie 'n uur terug te draai. Sal iemand kry om dit te doen - ek sal dan seker al slaap. Die pubs mag net tot half-twee op 'n Sondagoggend drank bedien. Dis daarom dat wintertyd 2-uur in die oggend inskop en nie om middernag nie. Kan die Iere nie nog 'n ekstra uur gee om te drink nie!

Minder lekker om in die oggend op te staan, maar die sentrale verhitting – gas-*geyser* wat so van tyd tot tyd in-skop - hou dit warm. Dinge hier is baie beter ge-*gear* vir koue as wat ons ooit in *Sunny South Africa* was. Dis net as mens die gordyne ooptrek dat die grys kombers buite, jou soort van terugdwing bed toe.

Die gasrekening vir die eerste ses weke was toe minder as wat ek verwag het, so daar is (was) geld oor in die *kitty*. Sal seker verdubbel noudat ek die verhitting ook gebruik, maar sal nog steeds op *budget* en op *date* inkom. Dis net dat mens hier rekenings op verskillende tye betaal - gas een keer in drie maande, ditto die telefoon, maar ook nie heeltemal nie en ek het nog nie 'n elektrisiteitsrekening gekry nie. Ook nie eers 'n deposito betaal nie. Vir agtergrond: stoof is gas, so ook die warmwater, maar nie die stort nie. Die stort is elektrisiteit.

Het gister 'n nota omtrent 'n pakkie wat nie afgelewer kon word nie, gekry. Nuwe battery vir my *laptop* wat Louise bestel het vir aflewering hier op die eiland. Los toe 'n nota op die deur om te sê ek sal vandag, vanmiddag 3-uur daar wees om die pakkie te kry - brief het dan gesê ek moet teken. Kry toe 'n oproep so twee-uur vandag. UPS is by die huis met genoemde pakkie - sal sommer die pakkie by my by die werk kom aflewer. Sukkel nog met die diens wat mens (gewoonlik en ongevraagd) kry. Pakkie word afgelewer en ek het nou nog nie geteken nie.

Was die naweek see toe - bietjie verdwaal-verken en in Bunduran / Bonduran / êrens opgeëindig nadat ek eers op 'n *guest farm* of plek geslaap het (net so duskant Dublin). Toe sommer twee nagte in die hotel op Bundoran / Bonduran / êrens ingeboek. Mense *surf* daar - in die halfduim koue water / eende-Kaapse-weer - hierdie keer 100 Euro. Het een *dinner* ook ingesluit.

Wil sommer daar gaan bly. Mense is onse mense - luister na *Country & Western*-musiek, eet gesond baie en gesels as jy net die geleentheid gee.

Pragtig man, te pragtig. Laat mens na Henties verlang.

Sal bietjie 'n foto of twee aanstuur.

Kyk, hierdie lewe maak my lui en met lui kom daar seker vet.

Die dae word al korter en die nagte al langer maar die weer is nog baie goed hoewel ek so af en toe my *central heating* bietjie laat werk. Dis meer vir die lekkerte as werklik nodig. Die son kom egter al hoe later op. Dis regtig snaaks hoe mens dit van dag tot dag kan sien verander.

So, met my gaan dit goed. Ook met Elbereth in Skotland en Marinette in die Kaap. Die enigste ding wat bietjie druk is die finansies – dis egter 'n universele probleempie dink ek. Ek leef ook darem nou nie onder die broodlyn nie!

Ek beplan om Maart bietjie 'n draai in Suid Afrika / Namibia te gaan maak maar dit sal die tyd moet leer – het gisteraand na vliegtuigkaartjies gekyk en praat seker van so ses- of seweduisend rand en dan nog die geldjies vir 'n kar huur, ens. En ek het nog steeds nie 'n paspoort nie!

Elbereth en haar vriend kom hierdie naweek bietjie kuier – eerste keer wat ek die man gaan ontmoet. Het al met hom oor die telefoon gepraat en hy klink heel beskaafd en natuurlik baie Engels. Dis ook vandag, die 22-ste Oktober sy verjaarsdag – 29 jaar oud.

Michael en Marinette het nog nie hulle huis in JHB verkoop nie, so dit maak dit bietjie moeiliker vir hulle om in die Kaap te koop. Hulle het blykbaar al 'n offer op 'n standplaas gesit

257

en sal dan eerder weer wil bou sodra hulle plek verkoop is. Marinette geniet die skoolhouery by haar hoërskool baie – lewensoriëntering en is blykbaar die vakhoof of standerdhoof of iets. Lekker tyd van die jaar – kinders skryf eksamen en dan gaan hulle huis toe so die klomp onderwysers werk net tot halftwaalf en gaan dan strand toe om daar hulle vraestelle te merk. Dit klink regtig asof die Kaapse lewe vir M & M altwee baie goed doen en lekker is.

Die Ierse vrou, wat Elbereth en Marinette sê na my sus Monica trek, is regtig baie mal oor my (en ek oor haar). Ek is egter heel tevrede met die afstand tussen haar *village* en myne. Dis so twee ure se ry so dit maak dit net ver genoeg maar nie te ver nie. In elk geval, haar nuwe huis is klaar gebou en word nou geteel en gemat. Sal seker einde van die maand of middel November leefbaar wees. Die arme ding werk haar dood en slaap minder as ek. Sy werk nie net by die werk nie maar bedien ook die seun en Ma met alles – van wasgoed tot kos tot wie weet wat en ek word net so bederf. Soort van in haar geaardheid. Was ook in 31 jaar nog nie siek van die werk af nie. Is 'n meer senior posisie aangebied vir van Maart volgende jaar met 'n maatskappykar en het ewe haar huidige kar vir my 'gegee'. Ek skop egter kwaai vas. Sal haar beslis saambring S.A. toe as ek volgende Maart daar uit kom.

Verder is hier nie regtig nuus nie. Volgende week is Halloween en dit is 'n groot storie hier. Ek stel nie regtig belang nie – sal net by my huisie buite die dorp bly die 31ste en televisie kyk. Ek is mal oor my huis. Julle sal moet kom kuier – silwerskoon beddegoed en handdoeke, tuisgemaakte kos. Ek is regtig baie *domesticated* en anders as in S.A., mens het tyd vir al die dingetjies. Niemand gaan ook voor elf in die aand slaap nie (en dan staan ek so net voor agt op nou in die amper-winter).

Mooi kyk na julle en die klomp om julle – ons word ouer.

The wedding vows

I Wynand Johannes Wentzel, take you, Linda Joyce Boyd, to be my wife, my partner in life and my one true love.

I will cherish our union and love you more each day than I did before.

I will trust you and respect you, laugh with you and cry with you, loving you faithfully through good times and bad, regardless of the obstacles we face together.

I give you my hand, my heart, and my love, from this day forward for as long as we both shall live.

Mauritius - 2 April 2011

Printed in Dunstable, United Kingdom

65473575R00157